Kindly given by

Jan Davies

for the solemn profession of
Sr Joseph of Divine Love.

Please pray for
our benefactors.

EPILOGUE

THE GLORY OF THE LORD:
A THEOLOGICAL AESTHETICS

THEO-DRAMA

THEO-LOGIC

EPILOGUE

HANS URS VON BALTHASAR

EPILOGUE

Translated by Edward T. Oakes, S.J.

IGNATIUS PRESS   SAN FRANCISCO

Title of the German original: *Epilog*
© 1987 by Johannes Verlag Einsiedeln, Trier

Cover design by Roxanne Mei Lum

ISBN 0–89870–281–x
Library of Congress Control Number 2004114782
Printed in the United States of America ⊗

CONTENTS

ABBREVIATIONS

FOREWORD

This *Epilogue* to my trilogy has been written to afford the weary reader something like an overview of the whole enterprise. It was after all a large project (now swollen to sixteen volumes). The reason it grew to such an ungainly size is because it sought to treat such sweeping topics as "aesthetics", "theo-drama", and "theo-logic" in a manner sufficient to such large themes. But this overview does *not* mean to offer the reader a kind of *Reader's Digest* of the whole, that is, a condensed, summary version of the trilogy. Rather, it wants to explain *why* the trilogy has tried to present theology from the perspective of the Platonic transcendentals instead of, as used to be done, in the traditional tractate style (*loci* theology, as it was called). Meaning simply this: How might we make the smoothest transition from a true (and thereby religious) philosophy to biblical revelation? Hence the title of part 2 of the *Epilogue*, "Threshold", where we will try to effect this transition.

But before reaching this threshold we must first pursue an indispensable, albeit insufficient, kind of apologetic: the Bible and Christianity compete for adherents within an abundant marketplace of religious wares. At first glance, these goods seem to jostle with each other on the same level of exchange, differing only in price and mortgage rates, so to speak, but all requiring the same legal tender. More deeply considered, however, they all obviously operate with different currencies and rates of exchange, forming, as it were, a hierarchy of meanings and interpretations. So one can try to show that the less comprehensive interpretations can be accommodated within the more comprehensive. But if we can manage to show that, the result will then obviously prompt the question of where one might find the highest integration. The seeker after truth cannot dispense with this method; but if it is to be finally fruitful for him, he cannot dispense with what has been developed in the *Aesthetics*. Hence the title of part 1: "Forecourt".

But what lies past the threshold? These are the so-called "mysteries of Christianity", which cannot be derived from any

9

religious philosophy. Given the confines of this *Epilogue*, these
mysteries can obviously only be delineated here in meager out-
lines, leaving out so much that is necessary for understanding
them. For that, one can always mine the immense riches of theology from the past two thousand years of the Church's theology
on one's own.

So a great deal that we have treated extensively elsewhere will
not be mentioned here. There is, for example, nothing here in
this concluding volume on prayer, nothing on Christian life as
theoria and *praxis*, nothing on person and mission, on the states
of life within the Church; but also no tract on Trinity, Christology, Mariology, or on the great figures of the Church: saints,
theologians, and so forth. Why say again what has already been
said? So let us just let this *Epilogue* be what the old French ballads
call an *envoi*.

Now whether this concluding word has much to say for catechesis and for the teaching mission of the Church in the face
of the kind of society and civilization as we encounter them today I sincerely doubt. The slogan is much bruited about these
days that we should try to meet modern man "where he is".
According to one report, "in America an adolescent by the time
he has reached the age of seventeen has on average sat in front
of a television set for 15,000 hours, the equivalent of almost
two full years." Here in Europe, according to a recent study,
children even as early as three- to six-year-olds sit before the TV
screen on an average of five to six hours a week, and ten- to
thirteen-year-olds devote more than twelve hours a week to it.
Hans Meier quite justifiably wonders aloud "whether, in this
age of the media, we are handing on a cultural legacy (and a
religious faith)" and, if we are not, "whether we will not finally
lose, with the lost language, our very ability to hear and see anything at all".

So severe is this situation that most teachers of religion ask,
with equal justice, just who these ruins are whom we should try
to "meet" (against their will!) "where they are". A missionary
toiling in the savannas of Africa or on the atolls of the Pacific has
it relatively easy: he encounters a perhaps primitive *anima natu-
raliter christiana*. What might come across to the native as pure

theological Chinese he can easily translate into the simplest of languages. But where is the famous "point of contact" with the *anima technica vacua*? I for one certainly do not know. Some table-rapping, a séance or two, some dabbling in Zen meditation, a smattering of liberation theology: enough.

This little work can hardly be more than a bottle thrown into the sea. To find land and to have someone actually come across it, now that would be a miracle. But sometimes even miracles happen.

I. FORECOURT

I

INTEGRATION AS METHOD?

In the midst of the abundant number of choices for adopting a world view currently available today, the possibility of being a Christian is but one option among many. Now the Christian religion cannot thrust itself into first place, for this would contradict the spirit of its Founder and of its best representatives. It must seek to establish its credibility and, according to its own understanding, its uniqueness with purely spiritual/intellectual arguments that, paradoxically enough, must not come across as so "compelling" as to vitiate the act of free faith and free self-surrender. It must first get into line with the contenders, each one of which makes its claim to comprehensive truth, or at least to being right. And then, from its place, Christianity must test the validity of all these claims in line and acknowledge their portion of the truth as a relative one. In this way, from the Christian standpoint, something like a stepladder of admissible truths will arise that can be arranged according to the well-known German proverb, "Wer mehr Wahrheit sieht, hat mehr recht" (Whoever sees more of the truth is more profoundly right).

This approach corresponds to the early Christian doctrine of the *logoi spermatikoi* that are scattered throughout the entire cultural and intellectual world of humanity. However, this doctrine should not be taken in such a way as to imply that mutually exclusive doctrines and points of view could have an equal share in this scattered Logos (for then the Logos would thus have to be continually contradicting itself). Rather, it means that the less extensive views are integrated into more comprehensive ones. Thus, whoever could integrate the most truth in this vision would have claim to the highest attainable truth. He would be—if one might cite here a statement of Paul taken out of its proper context—that spiritual man who can judge everything but who himself is judged by no one (1 Cor 2:15), because no one but he possesses so comprehensive a view of the truth.

But with such a naïve conception of "apologetics", the Christian spiritual mountain climber soon comes up against an impassable crevasse. To be sure, he manages to attain a certain height using this method of summation and integration, but he suddenly sees that, if he were to keep on following this path (presuming it were even accessible), he would come, not to Christ, but to Hegel. That is, he would reach "absolute knowing", which absorbs the Christian faith into itself (perhaps *optima fide*, in the best of faith), even though Hegel admits that this knowing needs, for its final synthesis between God and the world, a Christology, which for Hegel means a *speculative* Good Friday and a *speculative* Pentecost.

Now many Christians are of the opinion (perhaps with Hegel himself?) that they have in this way reached the deepest meaning of their own religion, but they do not see that they have, in so doing, missed God's freedom in his self-revelation and the ungraspability of the love that freely gives of itself ("only love is credible"). Without realizing it, they have got beyond this love, have put it behind them or pocketed it away, instead of seeing it always before them as a mystery worthy of their worship.

So what is to be done? We cannot simply renounce the method of increasing integration if we are to be ready at all times "to make a defense" of our faith (1 Pet 3:15). But this method by itself is not qualified to lead to the goal, nor would it be suitable even if it took into account the aspect of God's increasing freedom. For even then the historical revelation of God culminating in Christ could not be deduced or even postulated. This incapacity will, however, after a little reflection, appear as something positive. For the weight of the pure, underivable facticity of the historical proves so heavy in world history and in the world views developed in it that facts defy every attempt to string them into a necklace of ideas.

Both these aspects, the ideal and the historical, which at first sight seem irreconcilable, will have to be united if Christian reality is to be neither flattened out rationalistically nor dissipated into sheer irrationality. Attempts are of course made—based on the facticity of the Christian reality—to renounce all immanent paths of integration. Whoever joins Karl Barth in defining the fact of the covenant as the inner ground of creation must interpret creation as capable on its own—that is, outside the contours of the covenant—of bringing forth only the most varied idols, which for all their variety are, in their true worth, all equally vain. These idols in turn can be liberated from their reprobation only by Christ's act of self-surrender on the Cross, where they are reduced to nothing before the One who alone was truly rejected and made reprobate.

Less radical, but similar in intent, was the connection Schelling made between (tragic) mythology and (positive) revelation, since here a total reversal brought about by revelation seemed reconcilable with a certain graduated sequence of myths. (Eugen Drewermann today revives an analogous strategy by simply equating myth and the Christian Logos, both equally embedded as archetypes in man.) In a way that, viewed from afar, is comparable to Barth's project, Karl Rahner, with the help of his "supernatural existential", can portray the one central fact of Christian revelation as extending over the whole history of mankind—which obviously means that the "categorially" [*kategorial*] different outward forms of religions and world views then acquire only a secondary significance.

These and similar approaches place us before the aforementioned impasse: How can a method that proceeds by integrating isolated points of view move toward a unique revelation that is *independent of the event of creation*? Should we presume to agree with Augustine and Thomas that a dynamism placed within the original form of the created spirit aspires to the vision of God and inspires "blindly groping" attempts (Acts 17:27) to reach God? That these tentative searchings, supported and accompanied in turn by an already present grace (or by a supernatural existential), aim toward what cannot be constructed from the starting point of nature? That nature can then be taken up into a higher level by a revelation decided upon by God's free initiative and that both directs and fulfills that search at the same time? "Gratia non destruit sed elevat et perficit naturam" [Grace does not destroy but elevates and perfects nature]. Which of course also implies: "sanans naturam aegrotam" [healing a diseased nature].

If that is the tack we choose to take, then we must give up the hypothesis of a *natura pura* as well and, with that rejection, make two simultaneous presuppositions: the apparent paradox of a nature directed toward reaching God but whose natural powers render that goal unattainable and—trumping this paradox—the grace of God's self-disclosure inserted into an already "purely natural" freedom, a grace whose irradiation would be thought of as flowing out into the whole of history from its christological center.

Once this is presupposed, we could venture an (apologetic) integration of proposed world views within history. However, for that to succeed, we would have to bear in mind two things from the outset. First, even when, as often happens, viewpoints are diametrically opposed to one another on their own level and at least provisionally exclude integration (and thus block the way to a unified vision that can harmonize what is legitimate in each), nonetheless both of these viewpoints, otherwise irreconcilable on their own terms, could contribute useful elements to a unified vision when placed on a higher plateau otherwise inaccessible to either one when taken on its own terms.

Second, radical proposals that arose *before* Christian revelation differ from *post*-Christian views that consciously reject the unity brought about by Christ (as the center and highpoint of the biblical history of the covenant) and claim to have put something more plausible in its place. Pre-Christian and consciously post-Christian views might be structurally similar, but in their deepest intentionality they remain essentially different, since today the yeast of Christianity has penetrated the whole of mankind. For that reason, it would be quite difficult in today's global village to find something naïvely "pre-Christian" even in world views (in Asia, for example) that have apparently remained the same since pre-Christian times. Quite often they will have absorbed Christian (or at least biblical) elements to show that they do not need Christianity in order to maintain their own claim to totality.

2

THE UNASKED QUESTION

As is well known, the founding theoretician of positivism, Auguste Comte, forbade that any further attention be paid by philosophy to unanswerable questions—the very ones that the philosophical age just before Comte's (the very era he saw as now coming to an end) had so often posed. Henceforth, in this new era *of* the sciences, only questions that could be answered *by* those sciences were permissible.

It is astonishing to realize to what extent this program is still being pursued today, unconsciously or in some cases consciously, by ambitious philosophies and outlooks that claim to be fiercely anti-positivistic. Philosophy had always asked about the ground, essence, meaning, and final end of being as such (and about being human). The great religious "systems" had never ignored this question, even if they gave, or seemed to give, the most contradictory answers to it. For every religion wanted (and still does) to provide an answer to the question of the ultimate meaning of the world and of human existence inside that world. So to that extent, religion always contains the philosophical question within itself.

Positivism excludes this question and therefore consciously presents itself as atheism. But positivism has already, whether it wants to or not, entered the fray of the philosophy of religion precisely *by* stipulating that no question has meaning unless it can be answered, either now or later, by one of the "exact" sciences. In other words, whenever the question of God (and what, "scientifically" considered, is God anyway?) is rendered a priori absurd, the religious-philosophical question is both raised and answered, albeit negatively. Here belong all those presumptive world views that proceed from the pre-given empirical data "out there", whether it be the cosmos, whose laws are plumbed by science, or man himself, who is the object of medical, physiological, psychological, and sociological research, research that is rarely pursued for its own sake but more usually in view of "changing" (allegedly "improving") man.

Obviously, all the specialized sciences fit this description, but so too does Marxism in its many versions. Marxism customarily calls itself "materialism", but this is just a simplistic catchword invoked to highlight its reaction against "idealism". Actually, Marx's own interest in the essence of matter and the material stuff of the universe was quite meager. The whole weight of his passion was directed toward "transforming" the *humanum* to its best possible outcome, a transformation that he thought was being steered by an allegedly scientifically provable law of dialectic at work in the development of the human race. Humanity, as a sociological datum, is a starting point that disregards as irrelevant crucial features of human existence like death or—just as it did by certain social conditions in the nineteenth century—tries to establish their meaning as something lying off in the future.

In spite of his polemic against Comte, Marx's system is nothing but a sociological positivism: it simply takes humanity as it finds it and does not push its investigation beyond this datum. In exactly the same way, one can interrogate nature and its evolution (in the manner of Darwinism or other forms of naturalism) without so much as giving a single thought to the sheer "givenness" of nature, of matter, of life, or even of "evolution" itself. One can trace everything back to a Big Bang without in the least wondering why (supposing it took place) it happened at all.

Furthermore, returning to man, one can discover that he is the locus in the cosmos where questions about fundamental meaning break open; on that basis one can then construct ("scientifically", of course) an anthropology that describes the phenomenon of this questioning human being [*Dasein*] without ever posing the question of what meaning such a being has who keeps on searching after meaning. The object of this science is man as questioner, but it does not ask what kind of meaning he himself might have, even though man is the only being who questions his own being "out there" [*sein eigenes Dasein*] and, by implication, the act of being "out there" at all [*das (Da-)sein überhaupt*].

Only with this new question would anthropological science manage to cross over the threshold to philosophy. Then it becomes apparent that the various forms of psychoanalysis (whether Freudian, Jungian, or Adlerian) are inner-psychological sciences, whose aim is to "change" the question of meaning from an anthropologically inappropriate form of questioning to a "healthy" one suited to man. Even Jung's "metapsychology" does not escape this narrow way of posing the question. For the object of this science is still empirical man, and its goal is merely the rectification of man's attitude toward his own being; in no way does it question the meaning of being as such. (It is different in Victor Frankl's logo-therapy, which insists that the presupposition for human healing comes from precisely focusing on this question.)

We must raise an analogous question in an entirely different dimension of human history: whether Confucianism and Shintoism are anything more than a psychological-sociological ethic. Confucius' chief concern was to restore an ethical order in a turbulent time of Chinese history. His starting point was the conduct of the individual who, having achieved perfection in human goodness, has now become the "princely man" suited to govern others. This ethic is bolstered in two ways: by insisting that there is a cosmic order and by looking back to the great models of the past. Such an ethic is compatible with the most varied forms of religious belief precisely because it is ultimately nonreligious.

Similarly, the different forms of Shinto (state-supported Shinto was abolished after the Second World War) are hardly more than ways of maintaining the historical and national mentality of Japan before the onslaught of imported foreign religions (the mythological aspects of Shinto have long ceased to have effective significance), although this mentality can also be harmonized, as in China, with a variety of religious systems. It demands purity of heart, gratitude, harmony of life. The question of what lies beyond death is not raised, and the metaphysical question drops out of the picture.

But this question should not simply be the philosophical and religious question about "being *qua* being", as what we have just

said makes clear. Rather, this question also immediately implies
the question of the meaning or the value of this being that everyone can discern. Posed purely from man's point of view, the
question of being includes the search for a light that sheds light
on the meaning of man. But how is this light to be interpreted?
This light may, to name one alternative, make man aware that
the question of meaning cannot be posed; or if it can and even if
an answer might come from somewhere, he at least cannot get to
the bottom of it. Or, as a second option, this light might perhaps
hint at an ultimate meaning beyond and yet also somehow *in* the
totality of being. Or finally, perhaps this light may steer man
back to himself and his questioning, beyond which no further
meaning can be discerned or, at best, it would turn out to be a
meaning that manifests itself in incomprehensible ciphers. The
first "light" would accordingly be that of skepticism, the third
that of a reduction of philosophy to anthropology. Only the second would leave room for the philosophical-religious question.
Our immediate task, then, is to reflect on the possible forms of
this question.

3

THE QUESTION AS MAN SEES IT

Taken simply as a statistical prediction, Comte's diagnosis, or prognosis, has certainly come true: nowadays people rarely raise the explicitly philosophical question anymore. The age of science has replaced the era of philosophy. The "exactness" of the physical sciences is held up as the model for the life sciences and the humanities. At the same time, the aim of science is seen, with fewer and fewer exceptions, to lie in controlling or "changing" whatever comes within its grasp. Science subordinates itself to technology and productivity.

The consequences of this restriction are tragic: we get precisely the opposite of what we bargained for: slavery, not freedom. For technology does not liberate but actually enslaves man on every level. But these tragic consequences can occasionally, at least by implication, afford us a glimpse of the unrestricted philosophical question. Of course, given the current situation, that glimpse often enough comes mixed in with a prior despair or resignation. Or the search for meaning becomes a convulsive attempt to put the philosophical question once more between the pincers of the scientific method (through a thousand forms of the occult).

Now the genuinely philosophical question about the meaning of being as a whole becomes, when the focus is turned on man, the religious question about salvation of the whole. Initially, we may ask what form the conception of "meaning-salvation" of the whole can assume for man. Whatever else will prove true of it, we can at least say this: "Meaning-salvation" implies dualism. Even the most extreme monism cannot manage without negating *something*: for example, that becoming and finitude are a mere "seeming", which the ascent to the One must leave behind (Parmenides). But however futile this semblance is in itself, it has a certain reality for immediate consciousness. Even in the most consistent non-dualist systems of India (*advaita*), reality is impossible to pin down unambiguously: the world of appearance has to be interpreted away somehow: either as pure illusion (*Shankara*) or as the worldly form in which the ungraspable and infinite (*Rāmānuja*) appears or as the divine form in which the supreme divinity (*Mādhva*) appears; and finally, the *Vedānta* of Shankara requires the pure identification of soul (*atman*) and the All (*brahman*). But such a total fusion can no longer explain why a "semblance" exists in the first place. Individuality is what should not be (in principle it does not exist at all), and so the dissolution [*Auflösung*] of its seeming reality becomes redemption [*Erlösung*].

But this absolute monism turns itself upside down in the very attempt to be absolute: if this seeming reality in which we live counts as part of Being (or as one of the beings in the world), then its negation (*nirvāna*) quite properly bears the name of nonbeing. But if this nonbeing is recognized as the true reality, then what we call being, considered from that perspective, is nonbeing. The highest wisdom will then be—at least according to Zen, the offspring of *Mahāyāna*, Buddhism—to realize the identity of both negations and to live it out both in meditation and in day-to-day existence. Behind this conception is an implicit religious philosophy of literal self-lessness, a theme to which we shall have occasion to return later.

If, however, the seeming cosmos is understood as the scene of divine manifestation among men (*avatāra*), then we glimpse the possibility of witnessing epiphanies of the divine amid the passing forms of the world. These epiphanies can claim to be made manifest either in individual beings that reveal divinity or in a particular category of men like the gnostics, who discover a godlike kernel in themselves and seek to free it from its husk of illusory appearance and materiality. If this view is radicalized, the whole world of appearance can become a kind of organism of the divine, as in Stoicism and its many derivatives. Man must then try to recognize and live out in practice the identity between the "spark" in his soul and the great central divine fire of cosmic being. But this requires a leveling off of the differences among the attractive things of the world, for they are now all irrelevant to his inmost self.

Such philosophical-religious indifference is a constant in all the religious systems founded on this assumption. India is not alone in seeing things this way. Lao-Tzu's fifty-sixth aphorism says the same thing: "Not to be affected by fame, not to be affected by anonymity, not to be affected by gain, not to be affected by loss, not to be affected by honor, not to be affected by disgrace: this is the *Tao* [all-unifying unity]." A wise man of Sufism can speak in the same terms: "Of the various conditions like death and life, living a long life or a short one, plague and respite, fortune and misfortune, wealth and poverty—none really touches the essence of those who belong to the truth, and no outcome weighs more heavily than another." So speaks Dārāni. And al-Ghazzālī says: "His heart reaches the state wherein having and not having something are of a matter of indifference, . . . so that he inclines neither to give away nor to keep." According to Dāya, "honor and disgrace, praise and blame, rejection and acceptance by others are all the same" to the friend of God. Again, this attempt to live out an unrealizable monism rests on a conception of things to which we must return: in the form we have just seen it take, however, it destroys the reality of man in his finitude.

There yet remains a third form of monism to examine, *māyā*: the attempt to distinguish, within the sphere of true being (that is, the divine), an unimaginable, absolute sphere from a graspable, phenomenal form. This attempt attains its most supple moment when a "fate" hovering in the background distinct from the gods is distinguished from the world of the gods themselves (we see this already taking place in Homer); and it is in this latter world of the gods that man encounters the sphere of the absolute. If a patron god is devoted to a hero (as Athena with Odysseus), the mortal hero will then be irradiated with divine light. But it can also happen that the god will draw on the dark and irrational powers of fate, making use of them to drive the hero to madness and death (as Athena did with Ajax and Hera with Heracles).

Alongside this, however, there is the brighter vision in which the god emerging from the meta-divine background becomes the sought-for mediator leading man to the ineffable abyss of a man-abolishing redemption [*den Menschen auflösenden Erlösung*]. And when a god does so appear, as we see in many other instances of a mediated relationship of man to a god (*Shiva, Vishnu*) or of a man to one of his manifestations, the faithful who encounter this mediator devote themselves to *Bhakti*—loving participation, faithful discipleship, fidelity, worship. In *Bhakti* the faithful express their total need for a total self-surrender without wanting to trespass the boundaries of divine transcendence. An insufficiency in all forms of fellow-human love exhales a kind of air in this affectivity that—especially in the religion of simple people—forgets or ignores the ineffable and impersonal ground behind the beloved divinity. A *logos spermatikos*.

But whenever this happens, the god who thus emerges as an individual figure becomes incredible precisely *in* his individuality. What happens then is that people "see through" the god as a creation of the human imagination, at which point he becomes a captive to the mockery of real men (as happened to Dionysius in the plays of Aristophanes). The same man who had previously ascended into the semi-divine regions of heroic action now becomes the only one left on the stage, acting alone before the black curtain of fate. This is precisely what happens in *The Ring of the Nibelung*, a cycle of stories that inexorably reaches its climax in a twilight of the gods: as demi-gods, the heroes are tragic enough on their own, and so a tragic Wotan becomes superfluous to the plot. The supposed axis of the tale—who is guilty? Hagan? Kriemhild?—recedes behind the all-pervasive reality of the tragedy of existence as a whole. Here is where we feel the real center of gravity in the world of "seeming". According to Aristotle, a vision of this tragedy evokes shivering fear (*phobos*) and pity (*eleos*)—look at how a fellow human being suffers such a fate undeservedly (*anaxios*)!—and with such feelings of dismay comes a purification (*katharsis*, which perhaps could just as well be translated by "disillusionment": just as with existence!)

Tragedy's center of gravity was able to provide decisive support to the axiomatic Buddhist teaching that "existence is suffering." But this very weight stands in the way of the proffered solution that recommends a purely contemplative flight into *nirvāna*, a way that is in any case open only to an elect few.

That is why even in India there are two tracks or ways of life: next to the contemplative there is the active life (as in *Sāmkhya*, in the *Bhagavad Gītā*, and even in the *Vedānta*). But then, and more consistently, there is a second option, the thought of the compassion of the (personal) god who, although already mature and ready for *nirvāna*, postpones entering it until all beings have been freed from the tragedy of existence.

In its contemplative *Mahāyāna* form, Buddhism becomes, in Albert Schweitzer's famously tart line, "true orgiastic rites tempered by the desire to be compassionate",[1] referring to those superhuman, noble princes who imitate the god by immolating themselves for their suffering fellows. The forms of such vicarious suffering go far beyond, as images, those thought up by Euripides.[2] The thought of someone who is ready for blessedness vicariously suffering for those still burdened with *karma* guilt is something like a pointer in the direction of Christianity. The only trouble is that the dissolution of the Absolute into something ineffable and impersonal (that is, *nirvāna*) will immediately fall victim to Heidegger's critique of onto-theology; and the same holds true for the personal figure who stands before this looming, impersonal background. For Heidegger the "god" conceived as a person can only be sketched according to the model of beings in the world, which naturally can always make room for one more such being.

The final question, concerning the ontological status and origin of *māyā*, what it is and where it comes from, remains irresolvable in all three systems discussed here, especially if it is burdened with the overwhelming weight of frightful, ineradicable tragedy. Unless, that is, one takes flight in Hegel, where the Spirit pre-supposes the sensible world as a means to its own self-becoming. But as was shown elsewhere in the trilogy,[3] this system can do justice neither to God (who in Hegel needs the world in order to be himself) nor to man (who must be sacrificed as a concrete individual). Death is stripped of its dignity in

---

[1] Albert Schweitzer, *Weltanschauung mit indischen Denker* (1935), p. 93: "wahren Origen mit Mitleidswünschen".

[2] See our discussion in GL IV, 131–54; TD I 392–400

[3] TD I, 54ff.

this system: it becomes a speculative moment for the diviniza-
tion of God; but as an event of concrete life it is forgotten.

Finally, behind all the rich variety of these attempted answers
to the questions posed by man stands a final postulate, and no
attempt at finding a solution can do justice to it. All monistic systems that want in some way to outmaneuver the dualism already
there as a primal given (whether in the form of appearance or of
tragedy or of both) have tried to leap over an unbridgeable gap,
well aware that a still-yawning dualism would be tantamount
to a disastrous end of the philosophical-religious question. In
the religions of man this perplexity is expressed in their twofold
form as popular ritualism and as elite or esoteric mysticism. The
former clings to man's ineradicable distance from the gods or
from the divine, while the latter gives up this distance to attain the unity so desperately longed for by man. No religious
metaphysic sketched out by man can get beyond this impasse.
Strangely, according to Thomas Aquinas, it is precisely in this
dilemma that the nobility of man and of his questioning about
all purely intraworldly being finds its truest expression.[4]

This means that, according to the starting point of a philosophy of religion constructed on the foundation of human nature (considered from a Christian point of view), many *logoi
spermatikoi* have come to light, and some of them can integrate
others into themselves. But this also means that integration at
its most decisive stage is not possible, because postulates that
are apparently mutually exclusive are ultimately juxtaposed and
cannot be joined together in a metaphysical system that can be
surveyed within the realm of human question. Thus, if we later
make the transition to the data of the religion(s) of revelation,
we will already have realized that their data will not try to stop
up the holes that reason can never close. Nor can revelation, we
realize, help reason to attain to a conclusive system. For these
data are only valid for what they themselves purport to be: God's
self-disclosure in a freedom that can never be transformed as such
into material for reason.

---

[4] *S. Th.* I/II, 5, 5 ad 2.

4

GOD'S WORD

It begins with a Voice—just as a voice is heard at those abo-
riginal moments when other religions first step onto the stage
of history. But *this* Voice does not want in any way to be an
answer to the "highest question of man". Its sound is full of
living, unconditional, unquestionable authority. It speaks from
the very first moment with the demand for unquestioning obedience. The Voice does not answer questions but speaks measure-
less promise, a promise that presupposes pure obedience. What
is more, it is a Voice that apparently accepts in silence many contradictions: for example, Abraham's sacrifice of the son of that
same promise. The relationship marked out is the most specific,
concrete one imaginable, even if an even wider and more expan-
sive view of the universal has been disclosed at the same time:
"All people will be blessed in your name." The individual who
is addressed as one elect and chosen is told who he is (his name
is changed) and what he is to do. The relationship that has been
established from above is declared to be a lasting covenant and is
marked by a sign in the flesh of man. The "thou" resounds from
an "I" that presents itself for recognition in no other way than in
this self-assured salutation. If one asks for the speaker's name in
order to get a firm hold of him, no answer is vouchsafed: "Why
do you ask my name, seeing it is wonderful" (Judg 13:18).

But the covenant concluded by this Nameless One (for in the
meantime the individual man has become one particular people) is absolute: to persevere in it means life; to break it means
death. And it will bestow wisdom, manifesting how one is to
walk in the covenant: this is the gift of the "Ten Words". The
covenant is understood as the work of a perfectly free graciousness, a bestowal setting this people apart from all other peoples.
It is the graciousness of a jealous God who unsparingly requites
any presumptuous questioning of his grace. Whoever looks back
to Egypt while traversing the desert into which he has been led
by God, whoever murmurs against the provisions made for the

people during their forty years in the desert, does not attain to
the promise: "Not one of these men of this evil generation shall
see the good land . . . [even] you also [Moses] shall not go in"
(Deut 1:35, 37).

All other peoples were well acquainted with the gods and
would make for themselves a representation (an image) of them;
but this was forbidden to this people in the strictest of terms.
An image is a concept that can be gazed upon. But there was no
concept, no prior apprehension, of *this* God's voice. Every grasping for it will miss its object. This people and every member of
it were to find the covenant and its gracious wisdom sufficient.
Obedience was the guarantee of right relations with the founder
of the covenant. The bond that this covenant established with
God and his people presupposed absolute distance. Union across
such a distance was to be found exclusively in the covenant freely
established from above.

The "two ways" that were set before the people for their choice
were "life and good, death and evil" (Deut 30:15). You choose
life by "loving the LORD, your God, obeying his voice, and cleav-
ing to him" (v. 20). Perfect obedience required that the covenant
partner recognize an inconceivable grace had been vouchsafed.
Whoever did this was ready to understand this obedience as unconditional love owed to God ("with all your might": Deut 6:5)
and would discover that God's free graciousness was to be explained in no other way than as love, all the more so for being
so unconditional (Hos 11:8–9).

Needless to say, the other way, of rejection and disobedience,
is enticing: to be on the lookout for a god one can grasp, worship
in an image, and reconcile by sacrifice (and why not by human
sacrifice, since God has commanded the slaughter of Isaac?). As
we know, this way was constantly tried, so much so that God
avenged this disobedience with increasingly harsh measures, until he finally threw his people out of the land that belonged
to him. In spite of his definitive Yes to this bond, this jealous
God also knows a definitive No: rejecting every violator of the
covenant until only a "remnant" remained, a "shoot" that was
pruned from a "stump" that had been stripped bare. Even after their banishment was over, when the shoot once more tried

to act like a tree, they were brought low anew and forced to bow and scrape before alien peoples. Israel is the people whom, throughout its history, God has dragged along by the hair, forced to go where *they would not go*. And when, after all their failed opportunities, they were placed for a final and irrevocable time before the choice of "life or death" and rejected "the life", God, who "never regrets or repents of his promises", banished Israel once and for all out of fidelity to his promises.

It was not easy for a pre-Christian people to be raised in this idea of pure obedience as love; it could only come about by continually taking back what in retrospect had obviously been vouchsafed to them only provisionally. Take the case of holy war: God annihilated the kings who confronted Israel in order to make straight its path. Even as late as King David, God is still a God of victorious battles. But the people had to be weaned: so the enemy carried off the token of Yahweh's favor as booty. Although it was eventually recovered, the Ark of the Covenant was later set to the torch, along with the presumably untouchable Temple, because Israel had not hearkened to God but preferred policy and war to the required submission.

Then came prophets, mediators of the divine Voice. But soon Israel had to do without them, too. There was Israel's ethic— what people could get by without one?—in which good was rewarded and evil punished: but in this life. For the Voice had not delivered itself of any statement about a future life. But this, too, had to be taken from them: that one could not trust this law was perhaps the most bitter renunciation.

Job's cry is understandable (in fact even God shields him). Qoheleth's skepticism borders on the Egyptian and Babylonian variety. The psalms writhe in pain: even though they do not abandon the old law of earthly reward for the good, they still transcend it in their own halting way, in pure lament, which is sung right along with songs of happier, even jubilant recognition of the sovereignty of God. The poor of Yahweh throw their whole trust on him, the only wealth they have. For that reason, Israel's purest personification [*Inbild*] is the poor widow at the end of the Gospel: Jesus stands before her amazed: "Out of her poverty she has given everything she has to live on." No hint here that she did this in view of any recompense. She belongs, without knowing it, to the fulfillment of the great promise: "I will write [my law] upon their hearts" (Jer 31:33), and thus she becomes part of the New Covenant (Jer 31:31). After her deed the Herodian Temple can go up in flames with all its finery, and all ritual sacrifices now become impossible. The one thing necessary has been brought forth!

If this picture of complete devotion remains unique to Israel, still a seed of pure faith is also joined to it from paganism, as the examples of the centurion of Capernaum and the Syrophoenician woman show. But Israel's main path runs elsewhere. A motif that had only echoed in faint traces and was hardly noticed up to the time of Christ: vicarious representation. With Abraham this initially took the form of intercession [*Fürbitte*], then in Moses it was combined with reparation [*Fürbüße*], and it finally emerged as pure vicarious suffering [*Fürleiden*] in the Suffering Servant songs of Isaiah.

But it was two other motifs that determined the later history of Judaism (along with an almost ahistorical fidelity to the Old Law—as far as it still could be kept): first, the temptation to transgress the distance between God and man in *mysticism*. This can be seen in all those trends in Judaism from the mysticism and gnosis of the Merkaba to the theosophy of the Kabbala, its posthumous life in Hassidism, its rationalizing in Spinoza, which all finally dissipated in the relatively harmless forms of the Enlightenment and Idealism. But secondly, there was always the ever more passionate *messianism* that pointed toward the horizon of an earthly future. This often flared up in sabbatarianism and finally was secularized in Marxism and in its numerous Jewish varieties. Here, too, the line demarcating the distance in primitive Israel has been overrun.

Conservative Judaism might like to maintain this distance between God and world that mysticism and messianism try to overcome; but its much more successful embodiment and true world-historical advocate is—it should go without saying— Islam, which very probably is mostly derived from the last stages of a Jewish Christianity that was dying out and for which Jesus was simply a man specially endowed with grace. Islam sets its origin in revelation well before Abraham: according to Muslim doctrine, every human being has been born into the Islamic Ur-religion—that is, into the revealed primal distance between God and man, a primeval distance revealed by God, the Absolute One, out of his free goodness. Only then was the Kaba'a in Mecca (a city founded by Adam, according to Muslim theology) renewed by Abraham, not with Isaac, however, but with his son Ishmael; then this Ur-religion was written down by Moses and David and later extended by Jesus—who nonetheless declared himself to be mere man: it is true, he was born of a virgin and ascended to heaven, but he was not crucified, and he strictly enjoined his disciples to honor only the one God—in fact, Jesus had announced the coming of the last prophet, Muhammad (*Qur'an*, sura 61:6).

That is why, for Islam, Israelite monotheism, as a religion of a most free God who personally reveals himself, enjoys theological precedence over a dogmatically formulated Christianity: both the Incarnation of Jesus (culminating in the Cross) as well as the Trinity of God as the correlate of the Incarnation are for Israel and for Muhammad an absurdity and an abomination. Every bridge between God and man that is anything other than a direct, free work of God in inspiration or miracle—which obviously excludes sacraments, sacred images, intercession of the saints—is consciously rejected and cast off from the life of piety.

In the process, two Jewish features are discarded in Islam: the theological-national dimension and the messianic dynamism directed toward the future (the Shi'ite expectation of the last Imām is not comparable to this). This brief *Epilogue* can hardly provide a full description of Islam. Only two things need to be emphasized: first, Islam understands itself as a religion of the Book and thus values Jews and Christians as "peoples of the Book" who are accordingly tolerated within the Islamic commonwealth. The *Qur'an*, however, is always the starting point, which is why the primacy of Yahweh's history with Israel before the Hebrew scriptures were assembled and the primacy of Jesus before the formation of the Bible are not recognized.

The second point is the more important: with the rejection of the Incarnation and the Trinity, the redemptive significance of the Cross of Jesus also vanishes completely. Jesus' earthly life

ends in failure, but the point is that Christian faith takes that
failure as significant, for it brings hidden Old Testament themes
about representative suffering to light. Muhammad's life, however, ends in success, earthly success. That is why the propa-
gation of true doctrine can succeed using earthly means, and
in place of the Jewish earthly messianic eschatology, Muslims
await a paradise with earthly joys—in which God occasionally
shows himself. The faithful are purified, even if they were sinners, through a purgative fire, while the infidels await hell.

Nonetheless, just as in the history of Judaism after Christ, so
too in Islam the attempt is made to overcome the barrier between
Allah and man: for example, in the previously mentioned mysticism of Sufism. The complete handing over of oneself to the will
of God is tinged here with a selfless love that—like every mysticism that stands over against the undivided One—can only be
made coherent as a goal by this dissolution of the creature. Poets
can praise such dissolution, but where identity is taken seriously
(as in Junayd and his pupil Hallāj), that is the limit. After all,
Hallāj was crucified. Still, a great religious thinker, al-Ghazzāli,
arose, who managed to implant elements of this mysticism into
Islamic orthodoxy. But in Islam, what can the human person
weigh when set against God? Here the rationalism of Averroës
has the last word: all men together constitute but *one* spirit.

From the viewpoint of this Jewish and Muslim adherence to
the God personally revealing himself, it becomes possible to see
how exposed the position of Christianity remains, which precisely at this crux holds fast to its central assertions in both of
these passionately rejected motifs—Christ as incarnate Word of
God and God as triune love. What we said at the beginning now
becomes abundantly clear: the foundational axioms of a world
view and of a religion can be evaluated in so many different
ways that a purely rational apologetic of the Christian faith on
the basis of the principle of integration is not possible. Nonetheless, the attempt itself is not vain, and now at this juncture of
the argument the time has come to show this. We need not de-
scribe Christianity in all its contours here—its main accents are
known. At the moment it is only a question of how much it is
able to integrate the axioms of other religions.

Let us begin by comparing Judaism and Islam: Christians will unhesitatingly affirm both pillars sustaining these two religions: the ineradicable distance between God and creature (which is the creation of the free and almighty God) and the acceptance of a self-revelation of this God different from mere creatureliness— a revelation vouchsafed out of free love. These two pillars stand so firm that they resist every attempt at divinizing the essence of the self, of dissolving the substance of the creature—which is quite different from what happened in late Judaism and in Islamic Sufism. This drive to empty out the self means trespassing into God, something characteristic of the Eastern religions, too (insofar as they are religions and not simply an ethic). The reason for this drive is the inability to conceive how a finite being can possess definitive value and ultimate dignity next to an all-being God (or Absolute).

Christianity overcomes such uncertainty by its central assertion that God, in order to hold to the name love, wills to be *in himself* gift and fruitfulness. It is his sovereign will to accord space within his unity to the "other". Christianity asserts that this positive otherness of God justifies the being-other of the creature in relation to God. The "other in God" can even be this "other in creatureliness" without abandoning the difference of God/creature. Only in this way, it seems to the Christian, are the axioms of Judaism and Islam definitively established. Israel had never tried to reflect the possibility of an original and definitive relationship between God and man; while Islam had adopted from the Bible the Jewish trust in the freedom and mercy of Allah.

Christianity entered and filled the places left open by the two other religions of revelation when it assumed the positivity of the Other. The created spirit-subject now attains the irrevocable dignity of person. No longer is the people (in the case of Israel), no longer is the community, the *'umma* (in the case of Islam), the primary partner of God, but rather the individual (of course the individual is who he is only within the community), who retains his ultimate dignity by being a brother or sister of Christ. But from this perspective even the void of suffering and death— foundational aspects of finite being—gains an eminently positive sense within the otherness of being. Here is where Christianity distinguishes itself not only from the two "monotheisms" but also from every other religious view of man.

Where suffering and death were often enough what religion was meant to free man *from* or what remained as a residue that did not disappear and against which one could at best immunize oneself by a well-considered indifference, they now become in Christianity the highest proof for God *being* love, because Christ revealed God's love in himself on the Cross, took the world's guilt upon himself, and buried it in his own death. It is not a matter of proving this immense statement here but rather of showing that if it is true, it fills a position left empty by all the others: death (as torment and shame) is now ultimate epiphany and tangible, fruitful love.

In this way what was once experienced in change as negative (*māyā*), what was once seen in the ephemerality and perishability of earthly being as something to gaze through spiritually and to get away from, is now drawn in as something positive. The "superiority" over things as they are is now transformed in Christianity into lasting fidelity within this given and accepted mutability. Indeed, this fidelity to the finite now requires the testing of experienced change. Changeable material now becomes the test of fidelity's steadfastness, which is why the religious indifference of Taoism, Stoicism, or Sufism has been transformed in Christianity into a different kind of "indifference", that is, into an offer of *readiness* (as in the "First Principle and Foundation" of the Spiritual Exercises of Saint Ignatius).

Certainly this attitude remains something to be unconditionally striven for. But in Christianity this indifference no longer means trying to gain superiority over the polarities of honor-shame, riches-poverty, and so forth, swings of fortune's pendulum that assault the spirit and that all forms of non-Christian indifference try to obviate. Christian indifference, however, means to be ready to plunge into everything created, always recognizing that creation is something differentiated from God, fully aware of our experience of the difference. That alone corresponds to true creatureliness and has its prototype in Christ.

Here is where the great ethical systems of Confucianism and Shintoism are assimilated, since now it is no longer appropriate to transcend the human with a lofty world-superior indifference. Rather, Christianity encourages us to maintain in the human a "serene courage" [*gleichen Mut*], which is the root meaning of the word for indifference [*Gleich-mut*], a courage in the face of all that God has disposed, even the most difficult and contrary. And for a Christian this courage will consist, not in dulling oneself against such harsh realities, but in enduring and surviving them, acknowledging how real the fear, the disgust, and the wariness are that are inherent in these realities. Things scarcely possible to accomplish now become possible for the Christian, because now they have become meaningful. Even more: as we know from faith, freely borne wrongs join in the redemptive power of the Cross: "Whoever wishes to follow me must take up his cross."

Christian eschatology is determined by two affirmations: first, the affirmation that God is "other", which alone makes his essence as love understandable but which also can only become visible in Jesus' coming from God; and, secondly, the affirmation that suffering and death belong to finitude and contribute to redeeming the guilt of the world. Both of these determine Christian eschatology, in which everything meaningful for man and the world in the religions of mankind is integrated.

Such a double Yes presupposes a Yes to Christology as well; one that is built upon and is continuous with the Christology that is implicitly and explicitly developed in the New Testament and is guarded by the councils from Nicaea to Chalcedon: for only in Christology is the otherness of the world's being and the being of man (over against God) encompassed as such in the otherness with God, so that Jesus' Cross can be interpreted as the effective encompassing of the human in God's life of love without letting the created essence of man become absorbed in God.

This is due first of all to Christ's bodily Resurrection, the manifestation of what he accomplished on the Cross. By virtue of his Resurrection (see 1 Cor 15:13), he has gathered those who have been redeemed by him into the same bodily-spiritual totality in God. But since this happens through death and beyond it, existence "hereafter" cannot be imagined—as in Judaism and Islam —in categories of life this side of death. Rather, it is a transformation that certainly cannot be "de-physicalizing" but (for lack of a better term) can only be hinted at as "transfiguration" or "incorruptibility" or "the swallowing of death into life". Redemption is not *from* finitude but is rather an assumption *of* the finite (and thus of the other) into the infinite, which must have within itself, in order to be the life of love, the Other as such (Word, Son) and that which is united with the One (Spirit).

Measured according to the worldly forms of love—which in Christian revelation are transcended in a way that takes them far beyond themselves—one cannot say a priori that such a view of God, who can only be the One, is contradictory. Even less can we say that this revelation can be construed or postulated from the world. So God remains mystery: indeed, the Christian says that this mystery is not locked within itself but is revealed and sent to the world in Jesus Christ. This mystery can be accepted as true and thus can be believed as it reveals itself only in free decision, supported by God's grace. But in saying this, it must be stressed that this whole process of integrating all fragments of being cannot be a strict "proof" for the truth of the Christian faith. If such a proof existed, the act we call faith could be put behind us. But as we know, this holds true for human relations, too: as will become clear in the following pages, the communication of personal truths between two human beings always includes a moment of trust at precisely the point where there can be no occasion for doubt.

In conclusion we can point out a rationally problematic moment in (Jewish) monotheism. The one God Yahweh has entered into a pact with Israel, and he has so bound himself to this pact that he "waxes wroth" over Israel's infidelity, laments it, mourns it (as the Rabbis so drastically put it). Yet once again, touched in his inmost heart (Hos 11:8), he renounces punishment because love overcomes him. "Impassibility" cannot be ascribed to this God in any way. Is he dependent on his creature

Israel in order to love? And if so, is he then still God? One cannot philosophize about Yahweh without making him deeply problematic. That is why Jewish thought followed the detours of the mysticism of unity, theosophy, and atheism. Yahweh remains a God figure who points beyond himself to his own promise, to the God of Jesus Christ.

II. THRESHOLD

I

THE HESITATION OF BEING

The first part of this *Epilogue* was written under the motto, "Wer mehr sieht, hat recht" (Whoever sees more is right). It developed a kind of apologetic that forced the reader following the argument to see how limited was each level of man's various religious projects—and thereby to transcend them. Now religious reason chafes against this compulsion of having continually to transcend itself, and so it counters with plausible arguments against such pressure. These arguments can be mutually contradictory, even if each one is worth considering on its own terms. Because of this, there arises in the world of philosophy, and religion, too, an apparently irreducible pluralism that keeps forcing us back to our starting point.

But the protest against a particular form of transcendence can also adopt the strategy of deliberately renouncing this alleged claim to be able to "see more", thereby undermining the whole point of the motto. According to this view, the striving to see "more" undermines an important human attitude, one that seems to be much more appropriate to man, since it too demands humility, than does the proffered act of transcendence. Thus, to the Buddhist, it seems more fitting to maintain silence concerning the ground of the existence of this manifold and problematic world, which for the Buddhist is inexplicable in any event, than to come up with unverifiable theories. To the Jew and the Moslem, it seems more reverential to keep one's distance before the transcendence of Yahweh/Allah than to close the unbridgeable gulf between the Unconditioned One and his conditioned creatures at the cost of resorting to Christology and a doctrine of the Trinity.

Will not such syntheses finally and unavoidably lead to a form of Hegelian absolute knowledge, a dictatorship of *gnosis*? As the inexorable career of the historical dialectic has shown, will not such syntheses quickly lead beyond the real situation of man to the point of sheer absurdity? "Less is more" will then be the

43

slogan to shout to counteract the earlier maximalist motto that was once the ideal. Indeed, the *conditio humana* cautions against every form of conclusive overview: Does man really have to look on himself as the ultimate level of evolution? Must we really ascribe to the (Western!) personality so much weight that, to take but two examples, reincarnation or even a communist ideal would be disproved? Does not the actual condition of the world (Nietzsche's "ever-masticating monster") flatly contradict the phrase "very good" with which the biblical Creator characterized it? Does not the unavoidable mortality of man most energetically warn us to be humble? And is this not even more true in the case of every other higher life form, in which the fusion of death with sin is not even an issue? Does not universal mortality refute every search for meaning beyond death as nonsense?

Thus a Christian apologetics guided by the phrase "Whoever sees more is right" must let itself be interrogated everywhere by the meaning of this "more". But piling up more and more rational reasons for accepting the Christian view only forces apologetics into a clumsy assent—which in any case, if it is to be the assent of faith, must be free. For at every level of thought, apologetics is being kept from making further progress because it cannot help but encounter contrary reasons (at least hypothetical ones), which, even if they do not seem very logical, are still felt as genuinely cogent, existential objections. And these hesitations make themselves felt right up to the moment of a final Christian decision: and so one reaches the threshold, about to decide for Christ, and one hears, "Jesus, yes; the Church, no."

This often-heard slogan immediately encounters a deeper dilemma: It is not only difficult but downright impossible to reach the historical Jesus without using the New Testament, with its obviously ecclesially tainted redaction of his history and meaning. In the face of this snag—not to mention other objections that can be brought against the past and present countenance of the Church, split apart in so many ways—the decision to be a Christian seems to be the undertaking of a choice that can scarcely be justified rationally at all.

Confronted with this situation, we can find help only by radically inverting the way we pose the question: namely, by turning back from the question of the Last Thing—the purpose of human existence—to the question of the First Thing: to what is apparently the most obvious, the most unquestioned of all things: sheer existence. For, according to Aquinas, Being is what first encounters the recognizing spirit. But Being, which we always tend to presuppose as something understood, is nonetheless, according to Aristotle, also what we must seek to interrogate again and again. And what is first to be considered are not the subsections (the categories) but rather Being itself—which, on the one side, is the most comprehensive and thus richest of all concepts, fullness pure and simple (since nothing except nothingness can come from nothing), while, on the other side, it is the poorest, because every determination seems to be lacking to it.

Faced with this dilemma in the way Being manifests itself, we should not be surprised that it contains the most contradictory descriptions: for some, Being is the absolute, in relation to which every relativizing change is simply nothing (Parmenides); for others, Being itself is vacuous [*das Nichtige*] whose appearance (*māyā*) must be seen through, that is, seen for what it is in order to encounter it stripped of its illusoriness (Buddhism). Or less one-sidedly: for some, Being is what is reasonable, even in its apparently meaningless changeability; for others, change— the coming to be and perishing of facts and individuals—points to a superimposed sphere (of ideas) to which alone is ascribed genuine Being (Plato).

Or should we ascribe to change the value of an organic agitation within what is always the same? It would be inappropriate to develop here even a short history of these and other philosophical opinions. Yet we can still ask what kind of light can be thrown on this basic question of philosophy from the perspective of a Christianity that is at least hypothetically posited as the *maximum* and *ultimum*: a theological light, if you will, that can, however, illuminate the genuinely philosophical sphere. And in case this retrospectively cast light lets us see peculiarities of Being, which to us is so obvious, these for their part could throw light on phenomena manifest through them. It might be worth the try.

Our trilogy, presenting a theological aesthetics, dramatics, and logic, is built from within this mutually illuminating light. What one calls the properties of Being that transcend every individual being (the "transcendentals") seem to give the most fitting access to the mysteries of Christian theology. From these common properties, three were drawn out for separate emphasis: the beautiful, the good, and the true. We followed this procedure even though the transcendentals are indivisible from, and closely related to, each other (as will be shown in the following pages as well). In fact, they were chosen precisely because together they permeate all Being.

Before treating them, however, we will first take up the proper determination of the "One", as is usual in the treatises. But as the whole trilogy makes clear, the problematic of the One permeates that of the above-named three and is implicated in everything said about them. Still, it can be meaningful to treat the One at the beginning in a way that teases it out from the three subsequent transcendentals; and this will show at the same time why these three transcendentals, the beautiful, the good, and the true, were treated in the trilogy in what is usually considered an unusual sequence.

BEING AND BEINGS

If "to be" is defined as meaning "to be real", then a real being does not just possess within itself a part of being-real but has the whole of "to be", since as an existing thing it exists entirely as what it is, even though alongside it there are countless other real things. Essences are differentiated and divided from one another (a dog is not simultaneously a pear, although at another level of generality there are also relationships among all entities). But their being real cannot be subdivided; every entity has it entirely. Thus one cannot say that the sum of all things that have existed throughout the history of the world (that have been, are now, or will be) is the sum of reality. For, first of all, reality cannot be added up in a sum; secondly, many things could have been real that are not (the aborted child could have become an adult).

The sum of possible entities, then, transcends the range of realized beings. But possible beings are precisely not real, so that the readiness of "to be" to make hypothetical essences [*mögliche Wesen*] real is greater than their sum. In no case does an essence conceived of as possible have the ability as such to realize itself. On the other hand, however, what is yet to be made real needs an essence in order to become something real in that essence. Something real, that is, has come to be as the result of something else and can itself only then produce effects of its own. (A possible animal cannot move, eat, or procreate; only a real one can— and, indeed, does so—out of its own realized essence.) Hence the foundational axiom: "Esse significat aliquid completum et simplex, sed non subsistens" (To be real signifies something complete and simple but not subsistent in itself) (but only in individual entities: Saint Thomas, *De potentia* 1, 1). The whole of reality always exists only via the fragment of a finite essence; but the fragment does not exist except through the entirety of "to be real".

This becomes apparent when there is a graded series of entities [*Wesen*] in the world, according to which they become increasingly aware of their own reality as well as of their realized essence [*Wesen*]; or more exactly: they gradually become aware of the power (*dynamis*) of self-realization (*energeia*) given to their real essence.[1] And insofar as they can do this by virtue of the reality given to their essence, they gain a perspective on reality in general (which as such indivisibly permeates the whole world of beings): plants live unconscious in the network of their environment, while animals recognize their environment; and man is open for the world in its entirety; his self-consciousness is indissolubly linked with his world-consciousness—so much so that he attains to self-consciousness only as he is addressed by and from the world. In this way, *esse simplex non subsistens* finally comes to itself as spirit in the perfect reflection of human being [*menschlichen Wesens*]. Of course (and this will be shown more clearly later), this happens in wonderment: man is astonished that the whole of Being has been opened up to him, to the very one who knows himself to be only a fragment (in the midst of countless fragmentary beings in the world). The experience of reality is open to him, and he, too, at the same time is a being open from his very self to the whole.

Insofar as this is a highpoint that cannot be qualitatively transcended within the horizon of this world, we can say that the structure of the world, arranged according to hierarchical gradations (whether considered ontically or from an evolutionary perspective), essentially moves to its culmination in man. Now

[1] Von Balthasar is recapitulating standard Thomistic metaphysics here. The German terminology, however, does not coincide with either English or Latin. *Wesen* is particularly tricky because it can mean either "entity" or "essence". Also *Sein* is the nominal form of the infinitive "to be". The normal practice is to translate that with the gerund "Being", which unfortunately gives the impression that one is referring to a "super-thing", whereas the word in German connotes solely the act of "to be". Usually this translation follows the standard practice except where it is important to stress the infinitive act implied in the German *Sein*. Lower case "beings" (or "a being") translates *das Seiende* (literally, "that which is"), and "entity" always signifies *Wesen*. Because Von Balthasar rarely uses *Essenz* for "essence" (at least in the *Epilogue*), "essence" usually translates *Wesen* as well. In cases of ambiguity, and for the benefit of readers who do not have access to the German original, brackets will indicate which German word lies at the basis of the translation.—TRANS.

because the "to be" in man (as reality) is, in his essence, not only in itself [*an sich*] but also reflective to itself [*für sich*], man can be characterized as the "image and likeness of God", in which, as we said above, the *esse completum et simplex* must at the same time be *subsistens*. Of course this is only an image, because in the case of man this happens in an isolated substance [*Wesenheit*]. But still it is an image, because God's subsistence does not give to man *restriction* but—in contrast to nonsubsisting, reality-bestowing Being—*definition*.

But no worldly entity can attain the coinciding of essence and reality (*essentia-esse*), even in the case of consciousness, because it can never create its own reality but must accept a reality already given to it. That is why the freest entity *lives out* its essence in itself [*Darum west das freiste Wesen zwar in sich selber*] but is *grounded*, not in itself, but in what is trans-essential, in Being absolutely—not in the manner of subhuman beings that do not realize this, but by reflecting on what has made the human creature into an image of God, as we have said.

We should add a warning to what has been said so far. God cannot be "constructed" from the point of view of the world simply by equating an infinite substantiality with the "simple, indivisible, but nonsubsisting" real. For we recognize these two "elements" of worldly "to be" only in their respective deficiencies, which, even if both cannot be immediately identified, do not automatically disappear. Thinking about the two finitudes together (even the nonsubsistence of the real points to such a finitude) does not result in the absolute; at most it points to something lying out here beyond both. But thought is still unable to imagine anything about how this is so. That the spirit reflecting on everything that has been realized is characterized as the "image" of God naturally points in a direction where the prototype must lie. But at the same time this forbids us to fashion for ourselves an "image *of* the prototype", without which the image would not even be an image at all, that is, a definite being capable of comprehending itself and thereby also (potentially) all other beings, an image with a mysterious capacity for increasing comprehension of its surroundings but that those surroundings never seem to leave satisfied.

"The eye is not satisfied with seeing, nor the ear filled with hearing" (Eccles 1:8), says the Preacher. But he can say that only because, on the one hand, he knows of the unattainable longing for the fullness of meaning and spirit, of the postulate that points to the unfulfillable, while, on the other hand, he continually directs man back to his earthly finitude. All that anyone can attain here below is contentment and a gratitude to God "in all his toil" (Eccles 3:12ff.). This means that we must not absolutize anything finite (for example, the spirit in contrast to the body) in order to "construct" God, but rather we have to look out into the direction where the lines of our doubly finite being point. We cannot reckon how these lines are severed in the infinite. It is enough if we know that nothing finite, even if realized, has ever come to be on its own. It has for its horizon a ground to which it owes its existence: *principium et finem . . . incomprehensibilem* whose similarity points to an even greater dissimilarity: *Similitudo . . . major dissimilitudo* (DS 3004, 3001).

3

APPEARANCE AND HIDDENNESS

Reality gives to every entity its "to-be-what-it-is" [*in-sich-Sein*], and, in the case of a spiritual being, its "to-be-for-itself" [*für-sich-Sein*]. But at the same time it also gives to every entity its "to-be-with" [*Mit-Sein*] (because every being existing in reality is real through that one reality), and in the case of a spiritual being it also gives it its "to-be-for-another" [*Für-ein-ander(es)-Sein*]. For that reason every being has the gift of being able to "express" itself to another, which capacity presupposes an "innerness", an ability to communicate, that is, to impart itself. This "im-parting" implies a mysterious "partition" "in" another, in which the one imparting himself both gives himself away and at the same time—precisely in order to have himself there to give away—preserves himself. The "to-be-real" that is given to every being thus hides a duality in itself that might at first seem contradictory: (1) it is grounded in itself (which a mere being cannot do on its own, or otherwise it would be God); and (2) it proceeds out of itself by virtue of a dynamic given to it in order to real-ize itself (its innerness) in the very act of expressing.

If this expression results in a conscious being (an animal) or ultimately in a self-conscious being (man), then a really appearing being (whatever that appearing might be: a landscape, something living, a fellow human being) comes to perfection in its own reality according to the space offered to it. This space can be sensory perception or an assimilating and understanding mind or, in scholastic terms, the *intellectus passibilis et agens*. Real beings find completion in one another. But that is rounded out and completed when a perceiving and recollecting mind understands appearance to be the self-perfecting of what is self-expressive and not as something belonging to it, the mind.

In other words, its knowledge refers, not to appearance in its own inner realm, but immediately through these to the other self-expressing being—the "thing in itself". It takes the other *as* something other, not in itself (that would be a contradiction);

rather it interprets and understands the other's acts of expression as those of the other's interiority or subsistence. This is most clearly the case in intersubjective human conversation, where the word of the partner is obviously the expression of the other —who wants not merely his physically audible word but *himself* to be understood.

But because someone who expresses himself is always something more than his expression, he remains veiled to me in his subsistence even as he is a person truly expressing and unveiling himself. Only under this condition is there really something that he genuinely imparts to me—not in the quantitative sense: as if he could be giving half of himself to me while keeping the other half to himself. No, communication is qualitative: he must preserve himself as the giver in order to impart himself to me at all, for he, too, is one who must receive. "Preserving" here does not mean holding back but rather making possible the act of self-giving. The other person can, as we say idiomatically, "spill out his whole heart" to me, but only by remaining who he is and by not becoming who I am.

So true is this that I do not take possession of the other person when I take his "appearance" into myself—quite the contrary, I am claimed by him. But considering the matter from my side, not his, that is, from the one perceiving the other, this act of taking in the appearance of the other can only occur for me when I can gather up the variety of his manifold ways of appearing —voice, colors, movements—into the "unity of my apperception". I must "apperceive" the reality of the being encountering me. He is a reality I am thus able to recognize on the basis of my own reality. I am able to do this because I know that my being is not *his* reality. Rather, as reality, the other surpasses the limitations of my being for the sake of something infinite. Since I, too, experience this as a difference in myself, I can affirm to my partner the unity in the difference of his "being-for-himself" and of his expressiveness.

Accordingly, it requires the comprehensive, unifying medium of reality in order to "let the other be" (or to let every other thing at all be) in the unity appropriate to that other in the mystery of that other's "being-there" (whether human or object), a being-there I can never grasp. The other, whether a human being or some other object in reality, is thus revealed to me as a mystery lying well beyond all grasping concepts precisely when it reveals itself to me without any desire to hold back. By the very fact of appearing, the other is illuminated, but the eye of the spirit knows the light without seeing the sun that shines.

Insofar as the other (whether that other is a thing or a person) is revealed in me as a subject that never abandons its subjectivity, a fundamental trust of these "objects" shows itself to me in the act of imparting and knowing. Their appeal is to an ontic love. If objects are to reveal themselves (and thus come to perfection), they need an alien space, outside both subject and object, in which they can be safeguarded. This space is necessary, but it is provided in such a way that the objects occupying it are unable to claim this space on the basis of their own selves.

On the other hand, I cannot, as said before, affect the pose of one who lords it over objects (to the extent that I make possible their fulfillment), since I myself become aware of my own difference only by appealing to these alien realities. And I am given to myself as the being that is both aware of itself and at the same time of others in the comprehensive light of Being as reality. This light is all-governing, illuminating all finite beings [*Wesenheiten*] both from beyond as well as from the very depth of these beings showered with this light of Being. And this happens all the more, the more they become conscious and self-conscious —which means they can reflect that light within themselves.

4

POLARITY IN BEING

Now finally the problem of the unity of Being opens out before us—although it has always been secretly latent from the outset. By its nature this is a problem that forces us to renounce any effort to reduce it to a univocal common denominator. Reality (*esse*) can only be one (the thought of two "kinds" of reality is absurd a priori) inasmuch as it is *completum et simplex*. But on the other hand, it does not subsist in itself but in an immense number of entities [*Wesen*] and bestows on each of them its ontic [*wesenhafte*] (substantial) unity. Certainly, in the act of comparing, the ordering intellect can arrange these unities into genera and species. But neither genus nor species subsists as such. The only thing that truly subsists is that which is justifiably called undividable, that is, the individual. But even here a mutual self-giving reigns: Being [*Sein*] gives to beings [*Wesen*] its own indivisibility, while the individual beings give to Being (as a reality that merely hovers, finding no foothold in itself) its *real*-ization. Being is thus always both the most prevailing and general of terms, infinitely comprehending everything that is finite; but it is also the ever-unique. It is so *sui generis* that it cannot be categorized under any other category. A particular human being is unrepeatable. "A man's a man" might be a common expression, but it loses its validity right at this juncture.

The conclusion of our reflections so far—that there is a polarity to Being, one that determines everything in the world—opens the way for the rest of these reflections. For if the first (transcendental) property of Being permeating everything cannot be subsumed under some univocal concept, then the same must necessarily also hold true for the subsequent "transcendentals": the true, the good, and the beautiful—which can only have their place within the act of Being.

This polarity remains so mysterious because we cannot say that the finite entity is not itself also be*ing*. Moreover, one cannot imagine how the entity could have been released from the comprehensive reality to become the determined being that it is. This is so because reality as such—inasmuch as it is nonsubsisting and incapable of devising essences—cannot beget such beings from itself (for its own self-realization), especially not this entirely determined and limited array of entities that face one another.

This essential polarity of worldly Being, whose poles can only be understood through each other, inevitably points to an identity as ground—which, however, as we saw above, cannot be constructed from the poles themselves. For reality as we know it maintains subsistence only in finite essences [*Wesen*], and these are not even thinkable as essences without thinking at the same time of reality as a whole. This must hold even for the (inconceivably) infinite understanding of God, who can think up possible worlds that he chooses not to make real. Man as "God's image", and the whole world order subordinate to him, indicate that the absolute must be free spirit without our being able to conceive what infinite spirit really is in itself.

And yet there still remains an aspect of the difference to consider. For it cannot be asserted a priori that the difference valid for beings in the world (which could be described using the concept of the polarity of worldly Being) must be understood as a declension [*Abfall*] from the divine identity. If this difference really is the presupposition for the interconnectedness, communication, and mutual exchange among the entities, for their mutual inhabitation where they are conscious and self-conscious, then this difference forms the ontic first step of what love is among free entities. If love is rightly looked on as a perfection (since these beings always find fulfillment in others by virtue of love), then we can ask the counterquestion about the absolute identity of Being and essences: whether and how this intraworldly perfection can be grounded in love. An answer to this cannot be deduced by merely weighing the philosophical issues, as we did in the foregoing, because the *esse completum et simplex, sed non subsistens* of the world's reality can only point to absolute identity in a veiled way. Even less can the infinite variety of beings let us anticipate or suspect an all-encompassing subsistence of the absolute essence [*des absoluten Wesens*].

Only this much can be said: in the love between human beings a mystery already operative at the origin is foreshadowed, because the loving persons (in whom the all-encompassing Being of reality prevails) never close themselves off from one another. On the contrary, they are open to the original mystery of Being in their (always conditioned) fruitfulness. The fruitfulness they share, rooted in nature (as when a child is conceived) indeed remains an important but still limited parable of this fruitfulness of love, which at the most archetypal level must have some inexpressible analogue within the divine identity.

5

SELF-SHOWING

a. Every worldly being is epiphanic, in the difference just described. The life principle of a tree, invisible in itself, is essentially shown in the form, growth, and gradual decline in the appearance of the tree. In the variety of its phenomenal forms, the tree radiates its essential unity and thereby indicates the reality appropriate to it within the whole of reality. It has a *form*, one that changes organically, according to law, not arbitrarily. In other words, it is a form that proves to be a unified form that cannot be *trans*formed into something else. This phenomenal form of the entity is the way it expresses itself; it is a kind of voiceless, yet not inarticulate, speech. It is the way in which things express not only themselves but the whole or reality existing in them as well, a reality that, as *non subsistens*, points to the subsisting real: "The heavens are telling the glory of God. . . . Day to day pours forth speech, and night to night declares knowledge. There is no speech, nor are there words; their voice is not heard; yet their voice goes out through all the earth, and their words to the end of the world" (Ps 19:2–4). Or with the poet:

> A song slumbers inside all things,
> And there they dream on and on;
> The world begins to sing,
> Hearken but to its magic word![1]

Now it is the poet who "can express what each thing wants to say" (Claudel). Goethe would be more reserved, only averring that everything presents a "figure" that the trained eye knows how to read as a "molded form that develops organically". Again the paradox of veiling in the act of unveiling is at play here, or what we might call the phenomenon of referring: the stamped form inherently refers because it is something that has sense. If

---

[1] "Schläft ein Lied in allen Dingen, / Die da träumen fort und fort, / Und die Welt hebt an zu singen, / Triffst du nur das Zauberwort!" The poem Von Balthasar has quoted here was written by Joseph Freiherr von Eichendorff.—ED.

this were not so, it could indeed be form, but it would not be shaped by anything. The freer, the suppler the shaping form is, all the more articulately and in a uniquely personal way does it express itself.

This is clearest in human language. But as language also testifies, the form's very freedom of expression also allows the expressing being to hide itself all the more deeply: freedom as such cannot be seen directly [*hergezeigt*], however much it can point to itself [*angezeigt*]. In all cases, even in the purely natural ones, the epiphany of entities is their self-interpretation, it is their signifying [*be-deutend*], even if signifying only occurs by using signs as pointers [*an-deutend*]. And since entities place their signifying in a subject, it devolves upon that subject to express itself through the act of interpretation [*aus-deutend*].

As we will see in more detail shortly, since the subject manifests so much about itself that it can indicate as whole and real, astonishment is the first reaction—in two ways: (1) the unknown but real dimension is able to show itself in a complete and lovely figure; and (2) the subject becomes visible to itself in the act of showing itself to others.

A light irradiates the form itself, and the same light points to the reality that is both appearing in that form and simultaneously transcending it. The inner polarity of the transcendent ontic property of beauty lies in this duality of luminous form resting in itself and the innate tendency of form to point beyond itself to an (actual) being illuminated in it. It is not so much a question of the alternatives between classicism and romanticism as it is of the alternatives available to one's own spiritual attitude.

In classicism there is a greater emphasis on form, especially on that form uniquely possible in the world of art, while in romanticism the emphasis is more on pointing beyond the work to what it mysteriously signifies. But that question is not as important as the alternative in the subject: either to limit itself to the light lying in the pure form and appearance (that is what Kierkegaard meant by the "aesthetic sphere") or to perceive the indications of an epiphany manifesting the hidden reality of the light.

In the second case the beautiful will point to true Being, where the beautiful will be seen to be indivisible from the good and the true. Appearance can be beautiful even when it is divided from this depth and is merely feigning this depth in itself. But if this happens, then it really does become mere seeming. In order to be a radiant appearance, it needs the referential ability to point beyond itself, a faculty that, paradoxically, lies within itself. This is when it becomes epiphany. If the appearing phenomenon is denied as nonexistent, then seeming becomes the ultimate reality. Of course, this can still continue to mean various things. For example, if interest in the "thing in itself" dies out, then the "appearance" will become the only thing worth considering: it will be valued as something "enchanting". Here again we would still be in the "aesthetic sphere" (in which a consistent impressionism would also have to be counted). But if the Absolute, on the other hand, is recognized in negative theology as the inexpressible, then the appearance—for example, in the art of Tao or Zen painting—is liable to be read and seen as immediately referring to the mystery of "emptiness".

b. The recipient of the beautiful in all its various modes is able to interpret forms as totalities by virtue of the "unity of its apperception" (the form can also be a temporally flowing rhythm or a theatrically developing plot). The perceiver does not gather isolated impressions (the word *logos* comes from the Greek word to "gather"—*legein*) in order then to synthesize them. Rather, he grasps totalities beforehand in their appearance from the depths. The perceiver is able to do this in an intuitive judgment [*Urteil*] that does not subdivide [*unterteilt*] but apportions [*zuteilt*].

That is why something like awe is already there in the very ability to gather in impressions, since the thing manifesting itself is something real that cannot be absorbed by or expropriated for the ego. This awe and gratitude does not grow stale if one has become accustomed to the essence [*Wesen*] of the appearing phenomenon. Rather, it constantly belongs to the phenomenon of the epiphany that it is continually giving itself anew. "Just because you are, be close to me, giving thanks." This line from the poet Stefan Georges should not only hold true for the beloved but also for everything that opens itself up to us, for everything, that is, that is not completely formless (chaos) but that (humbly) offers us a form, however imperfect it may be.

And if the form that offers itself only radiates a musty, dim light, it still must not be forgotten that the act in which every finite being is made real is nonetheless the actual light of Being, a light that is also reflected in this particular being, especially when it is self-conscious. Thus we should distinguish in the recognizing subject between the unity brought about by the faculty of imagination and the unity of the perceiving reason. The first produces an "image" as its unity, one that can seem "significant" in itself and thus sufficient as itself. As, for example, in the aesthetic-religious images and myths, whose significance does not point beyond itself but rather lets the contemplator rest in his own light (which as such is already its "depth meaning").

Indeed these images and myths "refer" or point back—but, in the final analysis, they refer back to nothing other than themselves. Their significance [Be-Deutung] lies in their pointing [Hin-Deuten] to themselves. Thus whoever interprets the Homeric myths, not on their own terms, but the way the Stoics did, as reflections of the lawlike nature of cosmology, destroys them. In a different yet analogous way, it can be said of the Old Testament "images" that they "signify"—even though these images could be realities: king, priest, prophet, servant of God, temple, sacrifice, and so forth. But the reality (Jesus Christ) to which they point is not apparent to these images themselves. Nor is it apparent to the people who have been entrusted with them. They are Pascalian figures, meaning that it has not been revealed to them what they are revelations of.

Thus the whole existential tragedy of the mythical world, and partially also of the Old Testament world, seems to belong, in spite of everything, to the "aesthetic sphere" (Kierkegaard saw its culmination in the opera Don Giovanni, to whose eponymous hero women are only images of his Eros but are never persons). The fact, however, that the image points to a real essence being expressed in them can only be grasped on the basis of the unity of what Kant called "transcendental apperception",[2] which alone does full justice to the full concept of *Gestalt*. For *Gestalt* is more than image; it is the unity encountering the perceiver that is also simultaneously manifest in the experience of self (in the contemplated reality of the *cogito/sum*), so that the object encountered and the "I"—in spite of the variety of our ever-unique essences—truly communicate in the all-one depth of reality (*esse*). Only in the depth of this communication does genuinely spiritual knowing occur. But this does not happen by our purging images but in defining them as phenomenal forms of the entity before us. Man can attain to no more than what is revealed to him out of the depths. Or as Goethe says:

> Letting what is solid dissolve into spirit,
> As it keeps solid what is born of spirit.[3]

Beyond the power of the imagination [*Einbildungskraft*], but not without it, there occurs what can be characterized as "formation" [*Bildung*]: the constant, never-concluded, mutual process in which the recognizer ascribes to real things their valid essence behind their place in the world of images, while the things from their side do not simply populate the cognizing spirit with images but shape [*aus-bilden*] the spirit to itself. But the more refined [*gebildeter*] the spirit is, then the more authentically it learns to distinguish genuine appearance from superficial and often deceptive seeming, developing what we might call an intraworldly discernment of spirits.

c. From this transcendental epiphany of the entirety of the world's Being we can already catch a glimpse of the structures of revelation, that revelation of the absolute reality in whose midpoint stands the figure of Christ. In relation to this figure, the same twofold view described above is possible (if only analogously): we can read Christ as mere "image" significant in

---

[2] Immanuel Kant, *Critique of Pure Reason*, A 108.

[3] "Wie sie das Feste läßt zu Geist gerinnen, / Wie sie das Geistgezeugte fest bewahre."

himself or as the "appearance" of the One to whom he as image points and (according to his own statements about himself) always wants to point, and indeed must point, in order to be understood in his "reality". The historical-critical method, however, looks on him in the first way: that is, only as an image, in other words, as someone whose impact is on the same level as all other phenomenal images in the history of the world and religion. For this is a method that posits a problematic layer of potential "seeming" between the portrayals [*Gestalten*] of Jesus fashioned of him by his witnesses (which, being impressions, are varied and occasionally perhaps even contradictory) and the "thing in itself", Jesus.

How much "seeming" there really is here that is only meant to "refer" (in accord with the selective discretion of the witnesses) and how much, on the other hand, there is the "appearance" of the thing itself can be the occasion of a never-ending dispute if the debate is simply confined to this level. There are enough indications, however (these were described in the first volume of the *Aesthetics*), that this "seeming" [*Schein*]—without excluding the level of the "unity of the imagination"—can nonetheless be plunged into a deeper truth of "radiant appearance" [*Erscheinung*].

All that need be recalled here are a few of those indications: First, the variety of images (starting with the fact of the four different Gospels) is comparable to the various viewpoints that emerge when one slowly circles the same statue. Secondly, these differences only make sense when we take in all of the dimensions that the self-interpretation of the "thing in itself" (Jesus Christ) claims to offer: that he presents God (the Father), that he is recognizable in the Holy Spirit (Trinity), that his death on the Cross is the (timeless) reconciliation of God with a sinful world, and that his Resurrection delivers and fulfills the entirety of creation to God; that he has established the Eucharist as the foundation of the Church, that he has given her authority, that we are in communion with the saints and have the guarantee of his lasting presence in history.

All these aspects of the interpreted figure (to which we have only alluded) are indispensable if what is manifested before us is to be interpreted in its true reality in the way it intends. It is unnecessary to stress that the "de-formity" of Christ's death on the Cross and God's abandonment of him on Golgotha occupy a central place in this total form. Indeed, only this makes the figure perceptible at all (or more deeply considered: in a tragedy the death of the hero is often enough indispensable if we are to see the figure's aesthetic unity). But since Christ (as a human being who submitted himself to the intraworldly structures of ground and appearance) at the same time presents himself as the true interpretation of (supraworldly) absolute Being, this makes him utterly unique, so that the worldly structures of "form and light" (beauty) themselves serve as an epiphany of this above-mentioned structure of the Absolute.

In this way the twofold dimension of appearance and that which appears is explained. First, we can now see the necessity for Christ's Ascension into heaven, for it is necessary that the appearance *dis*appear, so that it is finally made clear that Christ's appearance really was the revelation of the *Absolute*. But secondly, it is necessary that the divine Spirit interpret this very figure as the uniquely definitive appearance of the Absolute now dwelling in Church and world, for that indwelling is now precisely one invisible to the senses [*leibhafter unsichtbar*]. Otherwise what has come to us as already definitive would be able to return in the same manner—a contradiction. Furthermore, if the (reconciling) death of the Son refers to itself as the perfect love of the Father for the world, then the already indicated analogous difference in the Absolute (which transcends even the meaning of difference) becomes apparent in God's identity. And the same holds for the possibility that a different Divine "Person" (identical with absolute Being) will enter the realm where the "to be" of every human person [*Personsein*] is grounded in the all-comprehending (world-)reality from which the individual "to be" of the human Jesus [*Menschsein Jesu*] will be "personified".

But this does not mean that the recognition and affirmation of this uniqueness result simply from the common property of being real that Jesus and believer share (that is, in the *esse non subsistens*) but rather that they must result from the fact that the absolute Being present in the person of Jesus must freely give himself to the act of faith from his own self—and that is precisely what we mean by calling it a "grace". Only in this way can the whole figure of Jesus as the revelation of God be seen. This does not of course exclude the human cognitive structure of reason from being taken up in the act of faith by grace, for reason becomes all the more effective, the more directly and openly it can approach the phenomenon of Christ: "To the simple it has been revealed, but it is hidden to the clever and wise." Once more grateful astonishment refutes barren ruminating.

One final thing: the intraworldly difference between form and light does not dissolve when one professes the Christian faith. But to be valid, it cannot be purely a matter of one element winning out over the other. On the one hand, we can gain real knowledge by sinking into phenomenal forms and concentrating all light on them (for example, when we contemplate every detail of the Way of the Cross on the basis of God's absolute love made manifest there). On the other hand, we can plunge directly into the infinite light of love of the triune God, provided that we never dismiss as meaningless the phenomenal form of God in the unsurpassably concrete, sensate patterns of the Gospel.

A moment of grace lies in all beauty: it shows itself to me far beyond what I have a right to expect, which is why we feel astonishment and admiration. This already happens in the simple realization that Being has already been "given" in an immeasurable, flowing fullness that is nonetheless poured into finite essences, coming to perfect realization in them. This is especially true in my own case: For I owe my existence, not to myself, but to Being (to my everlasting astonishment). But individual beings, as required by the act of being, fulfill their respective self-illumination and self-manifestation (as it were, grateful that a primal ground of being "lets them be") in a "form" whose moments are rightly and revealingly "formed" in an interrelationship with one another that takes place on the basis of a unity: that which converges toward a unity is the light as well as the form (in the event). The grace of Being that governs this whole process is elevated to a qualitatively new level, where the Absolute is illuminated and formed in the finite. What is demanded of us now, as we stand before this pure grace, which no longer reveals beauty but rather glory, is not to admire and be enraptured. Now we must worship.

6

SELF-GIVING

a. The transcendentals that permeate all Being can only exist within one another. A moment's reflection makes that obvious: for what is shown (beauty) imparts itself (goodness). Furthermore, this proves that even worldly goodness has a polar structure. This is why striving for something is universal: "Omnia bonum appetunt", says Thomas with Aristotle. Recall that *omnia* refers to all beings, "not just knowing beings but nonconscious beings too" (*De veritate* 22, 1). Yet I can strive for the good for a variety of reasons: because I need it in order to be or because it simply contents me (which can be thoroughly egotistical in motivation) or because I would like to have it as the good in itself—which of course only a free and knowing being can do. Only in this latter instance does the good come completely into view, immediately obligating me to become a person who surrenders himself. One can permit self-giving in good conscience only when one is ready, for one's own part, to give freely without counting the cost. On this spiritual level, the good stands as norm over the giver as well as the over the recipient (but who is also ready for his part to be given in return), and it governs the free consciences of both.

According to Saint Thomas, this spiritual level has its earlier stages in the subpersonal natural realm, in which man as a physical being takes part. Plants have a "right" to water and sun, animals to nourishment (whether from other plants or animals: the animal who becomes prey for food has no choice but to provide this for the preying beast). And man as a bodily being has a right to many things: to existence (hence the evil of abortion and killing), to all forms of indispensable physical and spiritual formation, and to a home that offers him the constant support of shelter. But man's right to this is not from his animal nature but from his human nature, so that we reach a paradoxical conclusion: at every stage of existence (as child, adolescent, adult), man has a right to love! Without it he could not become a human being but would otherwise turn into a wolf's cub. Thus he has a right to something that cannot be forced but can only be provided in free self-surrender. The paradox clearly appears in the line from Scripture: "Owe no one anything, except to love one another" (Rom 13:8), a duty that can never be definitively discharged.

Thus, in the rights that inhere in being a person, there always lies a form of power (and compulsion), inasmuch as a person always lives in community, for the human person will always be trying to compel something that essentially cannot be compelled: love. Furthermore, each person can be denied what he demands from the other—that is, when he comes across as someone to whom something is owed, as someone who represents all sorts of various demands—and his demands can be refused for reasons that are or are not good. In both cases, the inherent dramatics that develop between human freedoms, all the way from small family dramas to the total drama of world history, have their origins here. Theater is the place where this dramatic situation (as play, tragedy, comedy) comes to be presented, always with the implication that the audience will then go back and continue to play its part on the stage of life.

The first volume of *Theo-Drama* gave us an inkling of the immense number of conflict situations; at this point we need neither to extend its fullness and variety nor to expatiate any further on theater's inherently existential character. But one can see from the paradox developed above what kind of complications can result: rights of a lesser importance (such as right to the free choice of a career or to the love of another person, for example) can collide with rights of a higher validity and urgency. When this happens we are forced to ask: What does the higher norm demand, and what does conscience demand of those who defend these conflicting rights? What are the possibilities for adjudicating between the two? Is it the victory of the "stronger"? If so, does this mean the physically stronger? Might there be a spiritual solution lying somewhere in this conflict, or is that only a postponement of the problem? Or does it mean perhaps the morally stronger? If so, will the more morally upright person be able to convince the opponent of his superiority? "Convince" is a strange word here; originally it meant to be convicted in a court (whether rightly or wrongly), and then finally the word gained the meaning "to be turned to another viewpoint on the basis of reasons" (in which the question still remains undecided whether the "defendant" has freely let himself be convinced or not).[1]

As rights can be objectively arranged in ascending order, so too with the subjective attitudes about them. The former are *norma objectiva remota*; the latter are *norma subjectiva proxima*. This polarity, however, cannot stop there as the last word but must point to a higher identity in the Absolute. Here any use of force is utterly out of the question; what must coincide are rights (that is, justice) and love. Anselm has characterized this coinciding of rights and love: he calls it *rectitudo*. By that term he means what we mean by saying someone got something "just right". In other words, the term refers to that sense that something is right pure and simple and is balanced to perfection [*schlechthin Richtigen und Ausrichtenden*].

b. Proceeding further, the question arises in what way the good "acts": it gives itself—that is, its essence—but does it have the power to let itself be assimilated by a freedom? If it is truly sovereign, can freedom really be *in*fluenced from the outside? Let us recall the basic meaning of "in-fluence" (flowing in). Many languages know this image of a flowing out and over on the part of the good in order to "in-fluence" another person by flowing into him. The image seems deceptive, for nothing can literally pour itself into a freedom, which by definition is self-causing. For example, the whole apologetic that was laid out in the first part of this *Epilogue* mounted reasons to make an "impression" on the mind of the reader. But this mind is still at liberty to let itself be "in-fluenced" by this argument or not.

This is the whole issue for those world views and religions for which arguments must be adduced empirically from outside and not deductively, in the manner of mathematical truths, whose

---

[1] The German word *überzeugen* can mean both to convince and to convict. —Trans.

plausibility the mind already finds, upon reflection, operative in its own inner life. After the good arguments comes the "good example", that telling image that intends to exert a stronger, somehow more convincing (that word again!), more "striking" effect. Christ takes this into account: "Let your light so shine before men, that they may see your good works and give glory to your Father who is in heaven" (Mt 5:16). "That they may be one even as we [the Father and I] are one . . . that the world may know that you have sent me and have loved them" (Jn 17:23). Nonetheless, Christ in no way ascribes to this example an infallible effect; otherwise he would not have promised the disciples that they will encounter the world's hatred as he did, and indeed hate "without a cause" (Jn 15:25). This clearly means that the world will irrationally resist the most trenchant of reasons.

Thus alien freedom comes across as an impregnable fortress. But then how can Paul say he tears down defenses, razes every mountain that sets itself against his knowledge of God and "take[s] every thought captive to obey Christ" (2 Cor 10:4–5)? What kind of weapons does he use to accomplish this? In his "fool's boast" he points to his apostolic existence: it is a life that should "convince" because it is the copy of the existence of Christ. But he knows at the same time that this model rings true, not because it is a copy or "image", but only insofar as it carries within itself the form of Christ's own efficacy: "When I am weak, then am I strong." Christ himself told Paul, "My grace is sufficient for you, for my power is made perfect in weakness" (2 Cor 12:9–10).

That is why Paul is constantly at pains to avoid the "eloquent wisdom" of the "plausible words of wisdom" lest "the cross of Christ be emptied [kenōthē] of its power" (1 Cor 1:17; 2:4). Here Paul's way of influencing goes back to that of Christ's Cross, whose unique "power" will be discussed in the next chapter. But as in the forecourt, so too in the threshold we find certain human insights of general validity. For example, there are those derived from Aristotle's discussion of the cathartic power of the tragic in Greek drama: in the depths of tragedy (especially when it is stripped of extraneous material) one gets an inkling that the act of perishing in self-surrender can become "grace" and "salvation" for a land (as in *Oedipus at Colonus*). There is also the portrayal of the completely purged character who can let his compassion for his suffering fellowmen work for their salvation when he renounces his entry into blessedness (something similar can be seen in the Buddhist vows of compassion).

Closer to our own situation are intercessory prayers: they cannot be fruitful unless one offers one's own self with them. In all forms of intercessory prayer, we are called on to renounce direct influence and to turn to a ground in which everything, even the alien freedom of someone I cannot influence, is grounded (since this freedom, too, has naturally not produced itself but was given to it). Of course, this "essence-less" [*wesenlose*] ground common to all beings might be, as always, imagined: it might be imagined mythically, as the divine primal ground of all beings, or a-personally, as that which sustains everything personal, or finally as transpersonal, issuing from itself every personal freedom (even the one that denies itself).

At this point the biblical idea of vicarious representation begins to emerge from within the Old Testament, welling up out of this common ground that supports all individual freedoms. This is an idea that will be fulfilled in Christ's Cross, which "takes away the sin of the world", for it will accomplish its mission from within this "hidden background" of all those freedoms that are closed up within themselves. We will of course have to guard against concluding that the Cross works from the outside, automatically conquering even the person who decides to reject this offer. Objective salvation must be subjectively accepted.

Nonetheless, looked at from the point of view of the hidden background where all freedoms are grounded, we find an unshackling taking place: those who are fettered and are no longer able to free themselves by their own power have been set free. This takes place when we become conscious that freedom's bondage in chains is neither definitive nor meaningful. In other words, an image of greater freedom (to choose the good) is presented to the rejecter (it is at this juncture that the discussion about influence, ultimately about the "in-pouring of divine virtue", gets its meaning).

In contrast to the idea of God conquering man, which would

be unworthy of him, Irenaeus develops the image of *suasio*, which in its ultimate implication already points to the Augustinian *voluptas trahens*. As Augustine explains in his classical discussion of this in his book *De spiritu et littera*, this *voluptas trahens* is neither compulsion nor allurement from the outside; rather, it is the exposure of the heart's innermost freedom, a freedom that consists precisely in love for God and neighbor. The image presented to us by the term *suasio* is one that implies our capacity for exercising the freedom that is most appropriate to ourselves, one that has been graciously revealed to the human heart by God's ground of love (the Holy Spirit). "Cum potestas datur, non necessitas utique imponitur" (Necessity is not imposed just because power has been given) (*De spiritu et littera* 31, 54). But without *suasio vel vocatio cui credat* (a persuasion or a beckoning to believe in), freedom has no power to believe. So it is "God's work" and a "concurrence [*Beistimmen*] in God's own freedom" (34, 60) whenever a way has been made straight for the Lord and whenever someone walks along that way, affirming the good.

This, too, is where the transition from the Old Testament law prescribed externally to a "law written on your heart and sunk into the depths of your being" now becomes visible, first mentioned in Jeremiah (31:33) and cited in Hebrews as well (10:16). The external *pre*scription now becomes the *in*scription of human freedom itself. But we must recall here that this transition can take place only when we sink into the depth of death on the Cross. Only this willingness to die makes possible the ascent of the highest freedom of the other in the very descent of self-surrender.

c. This points to the mystery of the Christian "kenotic power of the Cross". This is not, however, a leveling, enervating *kenosis* [emptying]. Rather, it gives us new power, that of internal conviction. Because of this mystery the prophet can say: "No longer shall each man teach his neighbor and each his brother, saying, 'Know the LORD,' for they shall all know me" (Jer 31:34). "For the earth shall be full of the knowledge of the LORD as the waters cover the sea" (Is 11:9; Habakkuk replaces "knowledge" with "glory" 2:14). This prophecy is fulfilled in Jesus' word:

"All [shall] be taught by God" (Jn 6:45, alluding to Is 54:13) and in John's own commentary on these words: "You have been anointed by the Holy One, and you all know. . . . You have no need that any one should teach you" (1 Jn 2:20, 27).

From this point of view, catechesis is not an imparting of unknown truth from the outside but a recalling of the love already poured out by God in Christian freedom, a love that coincides with this freedom. We should recall at this point what was said in the second volume of *Theo-Drama* (II, 207–316) about the necessary fulfillment of finite freedom in infinite freedom. Essentially this fulfillment can only happen within foundational, infinite freedom. But this infinite freedom itself, by definition, can be offered freely (graciously, as grace) only if it is really to fulfill the first freedom. If a law-bound necessity overrules these freedoms, then the interplay between the two becomes impossible.

In contrast to the "nonviolence" (*ahimsā*) of Indian religions, the "kenotic power" of the Cross of Christ essentially and solely consists in a mode of the self-"nihilating" person who dies to self out of love on behalf of another person; whereas all forms of the renunciation of power and violence for moral reasons since the Upanishads—in Buddhism, Jainism, Vishnuism—either aim to destroy the appearance of personality and to extinguish the thirst for Being (as in a "thirst for meaning", a "thirst for self-destruction"), or, as in Gandhi (who was influenced by the Sermon on the Mount), try to make this attitude politically effective.

Nowhere, not even in the "respect for life" that is expressed in the teachings that instruct one always to be careful not to destroy even the least of living creatures, do we reach what Jesus meant by his command, which he himself lived out, "Do not resist one who is evil. . . . Turn to him the other [cheek]" (Mt 5:39). This is because for Jesus what mattered was not a form of self-perfection or a means of gaining knowledge. Rather, Jesus' intention was to amortize all attacks of violence in the spiritual field, alchemizing them in the very arena that is the instrument of evil. For Jesus, evil is not only psychologically exhausted of its power when we refuse to resist it, but, more crucially, it is taken captive in its very essence. Vicarious representation can take place only where the blows are not only endured but taken over and absorbed in the *kenosis* of the person as such.

This is of course possible only when the "nonsubsisting reality" we spoke of earlier becomes the "space" for the absolute subsisting reality and so the stage where it may "nihilate" itself in love. And in this "space" this absolute reality will also graciously accept those who follow this love. Only in this way does what is called in Christianity "the communion of saints" arise. It is here in the communion of the saints that the most subtle forms of self-giving, of theological drama, occur. Here is also where it becomes evident that self-manifestation is perfected in self-giving. This is why Jesus can call himself the "light of the world" (Jn 8:12), which the various kinds of darkness in the world try to attack when "their hour" is come (Lk 22:53). But this they cannot do, since the closer they get to the light, the more they are transformed by it. Origen has described this in masterly fashion: on one side, the light shines in the darkness so that darkness cannot grasp it, whereas, on the other, the light—because it is the light of love and has no darkness in it—is able "to subsume darkness into itself in order to drive it out of our souls" (Saint Augustine, *Commentary on John*, at 1:5).

At the conclusion of this section, let us once more point to the polarity in worldly good—between objective norm and subjective conscience—a polarity that is modified for believers by the Incarnation of Christ, for Christ himself becomes the norm that dwells in a new way within his followers without their ever being able to control it. But this polarity is nothing strictly deficient but rather has its positive origin in identity. And so the incarnate Son is the gift of the Father to the world. And he is the Father's gift because of his "kenotic obedience" to the norm of the Father, with whom he is one, yet not identical—and this norm is mediated to him by the Spirit.

7

SELF-SAYING

Self-expression in speech is more than simply externalizing one-self in manifestation or action; it presupposes the strongest tension between perfect interiority in the freedom of self-consciousness and perfect externalizing in a more than natural mimesis and gesture ("natural language"). Indeed, self-expression is a free imaging, in which the spiritual subject can make known its reflexivity, relying both on language's prior social conventions as well as on the personal invention of new sentences. Thus, we can now see in what sense "truth" forms the conclusion to "beauty" and "goodness", in what sense the end must at the same time be the beginning. Looked at from an evolutionary perspective, truth can only emerge from within the horizon of the world at the summit of nature's development, at the place where human existence, life, consciousness have reached the depth of self-consciousness. If we are to be able to discover something about truth and falsehood, there must be something pre-given. As Saint Thomas says: "Quod natum est convenire cum omni ente; hoc autem est anima, quae quodammodo est omnia" (Whatever is born fits in with every other being; and this is the soul, which in a certain way *is* everything) (*De veritate* 1, 1).

But it becomes evident at the same time that, without self-consciousness, even terms like "beautiful" and "good" can only be imperfect, preliminary natural steps leading to what they become in their full unfolding in man, as was already shown in the previous discussion. On the other hand, self-showing and self-giving must also already be inchoate forms of self-saying, even before man shows up on the scene. But this is only conceivable when the things themselves (as Josef Pieper constantly stressed) are "words", enunciated by an infinite, free intellect. Theologically speaking, these "words" are beings that have been created in the eternal Word. But they are also beings (unconscious, conscious, or self-conscious) that can perfectly express themselves only in man, who has been given the gift of speech. So even

77

their epiphany and their gift of themselves include as indispensable moments their emergence into speech. Thus we may definitively conclude that the whole unabridged metaphysics of the
transcendentals of Being can only be unfolded under the theological light of the creation of the world in the Word of God,
who expresses himself in divine freedoms as a sensate-spiritual
man. But in asserting this, we do so without implying that metaphysics itself needs to become theology. That is why this whole
section of the *Epilogue* has been called the "Threshold".

a. Language, which by its very nature presupposes the tension
we have been discussing between a perfectly free interiority and a
perfectly free form of its self-expression, is only possible when all
of reality, Being in its entirety, is fundamentally open to spiritual
self-consciousness. Which means that self-consciousness grasps
itself reflexively as Being, as reality, beyond which there is nothing else except nothingness. It grasps itself as be*ing*—which is
always more than the sum of the finite beings that partake in
it. Indeed, this comes to light in their appearing and acting, but
only because they are grounded in the real that bestows on them
this light for their coming-to-light. This is a light that finds itself
once more in the light of the spirit, a spirit that recognizes itself
as really existing.

But now the things that come to light (as mediated by the human senses) are themselves sensible; and the human senses are
gates that are constantly open (and real!), letting the appearing
and self-giving entities enter into the senses and helping them
to unfold through the senses. The eye does not learn to see; it
has always been seeing, both things dark and things bright. The
ear does not learn to hear; it has always been hearing, whether
silence or sound. But to the spirit, things that really exist want
to make themselves known not only in images and phantasms
but, more importantly, in their reality, and this is especially true
in the case of our fellowman. And this only succeeds when the
mind [or spirit], conscious of its own "to be", can grasp these
existing things in the light of Being by means of images and can
address those images because they are illumined by this light.

The full content of this position would have to be more exactly presented through a fully developed epistemology. For the moment it suffices to see both insights: that whatever manifests itself as real does so in a sensible image and that the spirit addressed by the senses of the spirit can recognize the comprehensive Being of reality only by looking on the image-phantasm (in which the thing shows itself). As sensible-spiritual beings, we are addressed by means of the senses, and we do not mature to spiritual self-consciousness other than by being so addressed. We *re*-spond [*ant-worten*] with a word [*Wort*] that is spirit (the *verbum intellectus* or *cordis*), but also with a word that has always had its sensible correspondence, even if the vision of insight into reality as such precedes this answer ("simplex intuitus intellectus . . . nondum habet rationem verbi" [The simple gaze of the mind . . . does not yet possess the meaning of the word], *De veritate* 1d, 27, 2, 1). But as soon as we "think" in this light, we also "speak" ("omne intelligere in nobis est dicere" [In us to speak is the whole of understanding], *De veritate* 4, 2 ad 5). And because the claim as well as the answer is "spirit *through* the senses", the medium of our human thinking and judging is therefore speech. It is for us the sphere in which human beings understand one another and themselves. "The entire faculty for thinking rests on speech" (Hamann), which is why knowledge always presupposes community. Theo Kobusch, in his work *Sein und Sprache: Grundlegung einer Ontologie der Sprache* (Leiden: Brill, 1986), has given extensive treatment to this reality. He shows that this medium is the sphere of realization measured to man, that language is thus no mere *ens rationis* and *ens diminutum* but rather ontological reality.

This medium is always presupposed as something general when concrete understanding or expression occurs, and in the generality of this pre-given medium, the personal and unique expression can be introduced so that one can make oneself understandable to others. It is philosophically meaningless to speak of language *in abstracto*, without regard for speaker or hearer. Only a purely technical language could be so treated, and such a language remains an (inhuman) boundary phenomenon.

How this pre-given, already available medium of making oneself understood originally came to be is probably best explained

by the fact that the language enunciating free words has always
implied the (subhuman) organic structure of self-showing and
self-giving, drawing this structure into the sphere of the spiritual. Natural "language" was always available as material for
mental-sensate speaking. For example, even mimicking is a form
of mental communication, based on natural signifiers (laughing,
crying, and so forth), in which we can isolate the personal aspects of the expression. Thus the sensate sign can be the human
carrier of something much deeper and much more extensively
spiritual than it itself is, and can be understood as such:

> What they want, they cannot give.
> And people only give what they have to.
> So you give a kiss,
> Wanting really to give life.
> So you give a bouquet of flowers
> Instead of a garden around a house.
> You give a book as repayment
> For the wisdom of the whole world.
> All gifts are only sensation
> And images in a cave.
> Now that I feel all fullness,
> I finally know how poor I am![1]

But if a human being does not want merely to say something
in dialogue but rather to "give" himself ("verbum quod spirat
amorem" [the word that breathes love], *De veritate* 1d, 27, 2,
1), as we experience this in sensible words, then the "poverty"
the speaker experiences in these efforts does not need to be
something hopeless. Souls can truly encounter one another and
change places through the narrow passageway of image-bound
words. And because the senses are, as we mentioned, always active, this exchange, this making oneself understood, does not
always need to ensue through vocalized words but can also take
place in stillness and silence: one can belong [*ge-hören*] to an-

[1] "Was man will, kann man nicht geben, / Und man gibt nur, was man muß, /
Also gibt man einen Kuß / Und man gäbe gern das Leben. / Also gibt man einen
Strauß / Statt des Gartens um ein Haus, / Gibt ein Buch als den Entgelt / Für die
Weisheit aller Welt. / Alle Gabe ist nur Sinn / Und Bild in einer Hülle. / Seit ich
fühle alle Fülle, / Weiß ich erst, wie arm ich bin!" (Poem by Rudolf Borchardt).

other without having to hear [*hören*] the other's audible speech. For what is heard and seen and felt is preserved in the memory and still hovers there afterward: through the mind's ability to imagine [*Einbildungskraft*], man can in-form [*ein-bilden*] images in himself in order to treasure them in his heart. Here the reader should recall what was treated more extensively elsewhere in the trilogy (TL I, 164–79).

b. Language presupposes two things: insight into Being as reality and the freedom to express oneself. No one forces the free subject to inscribe his own distinctive sign in the pre-given medium of language (which alone makes communication between subjects possible). And insofar as the subject is free to express himself outwardly or not, he is also free to posit an inappropriate sign: he is free to lie or to tell only half the truth. We shall not discuss the other question here of how far the anonymous medium of language can be harmed by incessant lying and thus become unsuitable for inscribing one's personal truth using a language now debased by a culture of lies. But the question is real, because of course in the last analysis language is something that has been distilled by the usage of an indeterminable number of subjects, and perhaps even by their collective abuse and superficiality, to the point where language disintegrates into a generalized cliché. That "public opinion" in journals and the mass media has the power to conjure up the specter of this (perhaps fatal) danger is certain. Among countless other examples, the case of Jesus shows that a generalized prejudice (which literally means pre-judgment) can to a great extent prevent a person from being able to recognize a true judgment.

But we must pass over this problem. For the moment freedom, personal freedom, stands as the condition of fully realized truth. There is a much more deep-seated problem behind this freedom to express something that we recognize as true or to be silent about it, this freedom to characterize reality truly or falsely. The subject "discovers" Being only when the subject is discovered by Being. The *cogito ergo sum* in which the subject discovers the entire openness of the real in reflexive and free self-possession happens only when the subject is addressed by a reality that

manifests itself through phenomenal images. That means that
the reality of Being comes about in each case (in both aspects it
is the same: as self-recognition through being recognized), not
as its own possession, but as something given, bestowed.

At this point, perspectives from various depths come into view
that now also display the polar character of worldly truth. First
of all, there is the subjective perspective: the subjective act of
recognizing the truth. For this act is certainly the result of a
judgment, and in this judgment I concede to the phenomenon
manifest to me the character of a reality that points to itself in its
appearing. But, as we said earlier, this act ensues only if, while
being addressed by this real thing, I gain the intuition in myself
—in a flash of lightning—of "reality", in whose light true judgment occurs. At the same time the light of Being is granted to
me for my own action (*intellectus agens*), for the agent intellect
itself shines a light. Thus I experience the unity of the "gift" of
Being as something "made available" to me. Or, phrased differently: I experience my freedom as "more than appropriate" for
me to own.

This opens up for us a deeper content. In the discussion of
the difference in Being, there was no resolution to the difficult
question of whether Being's reality, which is unlimited and surpasses all individual beings, releases the limited essences [*Wesenheiten*] from itself in order to realize itself in them; or whether
this demands a positing of an absolute intellect different from
this act. Provisionally it can already be pointed out that the *esse*
is "bestowed" by God in order to release the essences [*essentiae*]
from himself.

However this mystery might be formulated, it is certain that
the beings realized in the world do not originally depend for
their reality and truth on the judgment of the human spirit but
rather on the free choice of an absolute free Spirit (for not everything possible is real!), on whose standard the truth of finite
real things, whether recognized by man or not, depends. There
are an infinite number of things that man does not know that
have always been true because they are grounded in the fact that
the absolute Spirit has measured them, even if some might be
known and judged as true for accidental reasons.

But that in no way means that the "idea" that God has of this individual and factually existing thing must be something general and notional if it is willed precisely as this individual and placed in reality. But the truth-recognizing human spirit does not immediately participate in this uncreated, originating light of the Creator, which is inaccessible to man. Rather, the human spirit participates in the light of Being that freely flows out from man's own spiritual nature. This is a light that in itself is impenetrably dark and only comes to be seen in its radiance in individual entities and thereby also in the individual human spirit. This should remind man's spirit that this light, so appropriate to it, is likewise given to it from the absolute Light.

c. At this point we can look back at the connection of the transcendental *modi* of worldly Being. Everywhere their mutual penetration was clarified, although they remain distinct from one another as modalities. The basic phenomenon in all three of them was their epiphanic character, which permeates everything that exists: self-showing (beauty), self-giving (goodness), self-saying (truth) were seen to be various aspects of this appearing. This appearing is a kind of shining-out that recalls the illuminating action of the light. But this is only meaningful when we maintain the difference between appearance and that which appears, for appearance without something that appears empties its identity into mere seeming. The entity in its essence [*Wesen*] is represented in its appearance. This re-presentation gives it its form in the world. In this form it pre-sents its sense-ful, logos-based content as something entirely intuitable. It thus also gives itself from within the context of the whole world so that it can be used (*uti*) as gift but also enjoyed (*frui*) and in which, finally, even its truth is proven.

As just mentioned, the three modes, considered from an evolutionary perspective, can appear to be arranged hierarchically, since (1) mere appearance is already appropriate for what is lifeless, while (2) self-giving receives a definite character on the level of life and consciousness (plants and animals "give themselves" as nourishment in a way that is almost exemplary), and (3) actual self-saying remains reserved for the human word. But human expression in its full range is not the only dimension that contains the other two modes in itself. Each of the three modes can also claim for itself a primacy, which our trilogy tried to establish. (This arrangement should also be contrasted with the inner relationship of the three transcendentals in Immanuel Kant's three *Critiques*, of pure reason, practical reason, and aesthetic judgment.)

In a great work of art, for example, the beautiful so simply dominates that its expressive power and its self-surrender to all who enjoy it become part of its (unrenounceable) moment of beauty, a beauty that can in no way be reduced to its practical benefits. If the beautiful is understood theologically as the manifest splendor of God, then the same thing holds true of God's revelation as it does of art: this splendor is also something that cannot be exhausted by God's surrender. Nor can we ever reach the end of our enjoyment, let alone succeed in analyzing it into words.

For its part, a complete surrender bears both these other moments in itself: self-surrender displays an inherent, irreplaceable beauty, and equally it possesses a unique expressive power. As something essentially free, self-expression—the word—is the most endangered of the three because it can be isolated from the thing itself; and—as the purely abstract language of "exact science" or even as empty chatter that says nothing—it can disintegrate into a distortion of its real identity. But genuinely human speech that carries with itself and expresses both the sensible image [*Bild*] and its inner structure [*Gebild*], as well as the self-surrender of the heart, can step out into the midpoint of Being's self-illumination.

Subjectively, the admiring astonishment that does not slacken when one improves one's acquaintance with the beautiful (for example, in a great work of art) corresponds to the dominance of the beautiful; while gratitude (that never "gets used to" the gift) corresponds to the dominance of the good. And to the dominance of the true (in its highest form in the human community) there corresponds the faith that does not atrophy with deeper knowledge and acquaintance, because it respects the unknowable freedom of God in his self-expression.

We have shown, then, that a basic polarity can be traced through all three transcendental modes. Furthermore, we have shown that this polarity is derived from the all-pervading polarity of unity that, as the first of the transcendental modes, undergirds all the others. And now unavoidably, because we have already met with the phenomenon of the not-one unity [*nicht-einen Einheit*], we must now encounter the question of the one unity identical in itself, and this means raising the question of the analogy of being.

The immense wealth of vitality that lies in the transcendental difference, however, permits us to analyze the question in a double form. The polarity governing everything finite (meaning, both the polarity of Being as well as that of its transcendentals) must be taken up, indeed superseded, into the absolute One, into *the* True, *the* Good, *the* Beautiful. Indeed the latter, the transcendentals, must so overlap and interpenetrate that each one could be emphasized for contemplation without the other two receding or being shortchanged. God's splendor *is* his self-surrender, and this once more *is* his truth. Nevertheless, this identity has for its presupposition the fact that God—beyond the highest form of Being of the world, of spirit—is absolute Spirit and thus absolute self-possessing freedom. This is a freedom that so pervades his whole Being that there cannot be a remainder of Being outside this freedom, nor could some corner of his Being manage to withdraw from this freedom.

And yet the self-showing, self-bestowal, and self-expressiveness of finite things are not aspects that arise out of their need but belong to their essential ontological perfection. Thus they must have their archetype in divine Being. What this might be only the self-revelation of God and its second-order reflection, theology, can say. Here "To Be", as perfect self-expression and as self-surrender within the identity, will be the personal difference of Father and Son, a difference that must, as love, have its fruitfulness as Holy Spirit. "Son" is therefore at the same time "Word" (as self-expression). He is "expression" (as the One who shows himself). He is also, and equally, "child" (the One lovingly begotten). And this personal difference must be overtaken in the personal unity of the different Persons, a unity that does not abolish these differences but rather unites them in the unity of the fruitfulness transcending the differences.

These are mysteries that cannot be deduced from the perspective of a necessary analogy between worldly being and its origin. On the contrary, they reveal themselves as everlasting mysteries only when God's sovereignty permits him and occasions him out of free love, out of free self-expression, freely glorifying himself, to create the being of the world. And thus this worldly being will then necessarily contain within itself traces and images of the intradivine difference, which means that it can then appropriately enter upon a union with the divine unity. These traces will then explain the ground and goal of this divine world enterprise: to show that, just as God can be one with the other Divine Persons *in* himself, he is just as capable, in his freedom, of becoming one with the others outside himself.

III. CATHEDRAL

CHRISTOLOGY AND TRINITY

Much of what was discussed in the second section about the transcendentals has in fact already led us over the threshold and into the inner sanctum: the actual holiness of the Christian act of salvation. This move corresponds in the trilogy to the way in which each basic property of Being points beyond its philosophical to its theological aspect. But this was always done in such a way that in the *similitudo* the *major dissimilitudo* would be clear—just as the "foolishness of God brings to naught" all the wisdom of man. But this *major dissimilitudo* would have to be continually revealed within the *similitudo* in such a way that man, endowed with the Holy Spirit, really could see that "the foolishness of God is wiser than men, and the weakness of God is stronger than men" (1 Cor 1:25), which, to be sure, rests entirely on the "folly" of "Christ crucified" (1:23), since the power of the Cross of Christ can in no way "be emptied of its power" (1:17). The paradox is explicit: the powerlessness of the crucified Lord must not lose its power. With this "word of the cross" (1:18), we have finally crossed over the threshold, and now we enter the inner sanctum, there to treat (to speak oxymoronically) the sacred "public" *arcana* of Christian revelation.

Entering this sacred space does not mean, however, that the "forecourt" and "threshold" have suddenly become otiose but only that the continuity of the Holy of Holies with the other two locations can be recognized by those alone who have crossed the threshold and now worship within the splendor of the cathedral.

a. How can Jesus say of himself "I am the Truth"? This is possible only because all that is true in the world "hold[s] together" in him (Col 1:17), which in turn presupposes that the *analogia entis* is personified in him, that he is the adequate sign, surrender, and expression of God within finite being. To approach this mystery we must try to think: In God himself the total epiphany, self-surrender, and self-expression of God the Father *is* the Son,

identical with him as God, in whom everything—even everything that is possible for God—is expressed. Only if God freely
decides in the Son to bring forth a fullness of nondivine beings
can the Son's essentially "relative" and thus "kenotic" act in
God be seen as a personal act (*esse completum subsistens*) within
the act of creation that gives to everything its real identity (*esse
completum sed non subsistens*). But the Son's kenotic life is not just
relatively kenotic but is also in its own way fully kenotic. Only
in this way can he assume the image of human likeness (the
homoiōma anthrōpōn of Philippians 2:7), personifying man in his
reality, but not, as it were, to replace the *esse non subsistens*, since
otherwise he would have personified the whole of humanity.

And so he appears in a human nature [*Wesen*] whose sensible
self-manifestation he shares and whose word, when he speaks of
God, must be taken on faith like any other person's. Can the
truth of what he says be proved subsequently? He himself points
to his deeds for this proof: "If . . . you do not believe me, believe the works" (Jn 10:38). "If I am not doing the works of my
Father, then do not believe me" (Jn 10:37). He means by these
works, first of all, of course the miracles, which cannot be explained through human power. But in a further sense his entire
human fate is intended as a lasting work stamped in the proto-
typical image of the Father working in him (Jn 5:19f.). This is
a work that reaches its summit in his death on the Cross and in
the Resurrection. Thus Jesus' whole human existence becomes
God's self-expression and self-surrender. He is so unique both
in speech ("A new teaching! With authority . . ." [Mk 1:27];
"No man ever spoke like this man!" [Jn 7:46]) as well as in his
deliberate silence, in his action as well as his Passion, that the
truth of his whole being can be deciphered both from his exalt-
edness (a manifesting splendor) and from his perfect servitude
(the "Teacher and Lord" of John 13:13 is the "one who serves"
in Luke 22:27). This is completely convincing: we perceive him
with a certainty that, far from excluding faith, includes it.

His person reveals itself so convincingly in his sensible appearance (in the three transcendentals) that he can say: "He who has
seen me has seen the Father" (Jn 14:9). But we must realize
that there is no question, when we see the way Jesus points

beyond himself to the Father, of *our* transcending this sensible appearing. For, as with other men, his free person manifests itself no differently from what happens in the case of any other worldly phenomenon: *in* this appearing lies the "image" (*eikōn*) or "likeness" (*homoiōma*) of the Father's archetype. Of course, to demand this kind of ability to see through the sensible image to the divine reality to which it points certainly demands more of human nature than it can supply. That is why we have been promised the penetrating insight of the Holy Spirit to accomplish this, who will "guide you into all the truth" (Jn 16:13).

But as Jesus as the Son of God had fully entered into a true human nature, so the Spirit will not remain hovering over man's human grasping but will fully penetrate it, thereby enabling it, together with the empowering Spirit, to see through the man Jesus to the divine background. "We have received . . . the Spirit which is from God, that we might understand the gifts bestowed on us by God" (1 Cor 2:12). This is an insight, to repeat, that includes faith as an act of trust in a way that is analogous to what we do when we come to know our fellow human beings.

We must still mention something about Jesus' sensible appearance. Insofar as he was a human being, his death and thus the cessation of his sensible manifestation belong necessarily to the truth of his being human. But insofar as he is the victor over death in his own dying, and thus has revealed the "immeasurable greatness of [God's] power" (Eph 1:19–20), he has been eternally resurrected in body, for his sensible physicality was an essential tool for his revelation of God to us. Thus both must coincide: the manifestation of his risen bodiliness before witnesses ("heard, . . . seen . . . and touched" [1 Jn 1:1–2]) and the disappearance of his sensibly grasped bodiliness without prejudice to his lasting invisible—yet definitive—presence.

b. But we should not overlook the fact that the *analogia entis* made present in Christ is in no way situated between, on one side, the intraworldly difference between existence and essence (and the transcendentals that pervade this distinction) and, on the other, the Being of God and his free ways of revealing himself (in which once more the transcendentals pervade, but in

their own way). Otherwise it would presuppose that we could
see the analogy in God directly. In other words, what seems to
be structured as a polarity in the world could be established in
thought as identical in God. What in the world only seems to be
finite and thus different from in-finite Being, the essence, would
in God be established as identical with infinite Being (which
as such would then be thought of as subsistent). But precisely
this identification of an act of being that we experience and can
conceive in no other way except as *completum non subsistens* with
an entity in the world that we encounter in the world as strictly
limited and defined would identify two moments in God that we
cannot conceive of except non-absolutely (as we already stressed
above).

So this attribution of such an identity to God would remain
a failed attempt to think in the direction of God, the very accu-
sation that Martin Heidegger made when he condemned onto-
theo-logy. The real "identity" of God that unfolds the vitality
of the transcendentals in its (to us) inconceivable way in God's
threefold personality lies—to speak with Plato and then later
with Gregory of Nyssa and Dionysius the Areopagite—*epekeina
tou ontos* (the far side of being), above and beyond what we
can still make out as "the 'to be' of beings" [*Seiendsein*]. Only
from this "above and beyond" that points beyond all order and
law-likeness of worldly being to God's freedom—a freedom that
nothing can overcome—can God in his sovereign freedom make
use of the most comprehensive reality of all that we know, Being, not so as to define himself ("I am who am"), but in order
to characterize his inconceivably free turning to us ("I will always be who I will be"), in contrast to the idols that are always
"identities woven whole cloth out of human thinking".

This transcendence over what we think of as identical (where
God is simply *causa sui*, the ground of his own self, an axiom
that only produces a figment of thought) is revealed in Jesus
Christ. Only in this way is God's perfect freedom unveiled as
an inner vitality in which the transcendentals are identified with
his identity. There is no possibility of separating the life of the
three Persons from God's essence. This essence is no fourth el-

ement, something common to the three Persons. Rather, it is their eternal life itself in its processions. This is why God's "Being" (thought of as a substance) does not manifest itself in the true-good-beautiful. On the contrary, the manifestation of the inner divine life (the processions) is as such identical with the transcendentals, which are identical to each other.

In this way the "good" now dominates as the central moment: self-showing and self-expressing culminate in absolute self-giving, so much so that everything self-referential [*Fürsich*] has already been transcended in reference to a thou [*Fürdich*]. To think in any other way would be Arianism. This absolute self-giving can only be a "begetting" (within the divine identity). And its result can only be a total acceptance of, and a total responding gift to, the origin. Thus the "love" of giving back in return can never be less than that of the begetting. From this we conclude that the interpenetration of love elicits that identity of love, equally powerfully in all three Persons, which is both the fruit as well as the "conclusive" manifestation of the absoluteness of divine love (once more, with all this taking place within the divine identity). "God is love" and nothing else; in this love lies every possible form of self-expression, of truth, and of wisdom. But this is a beauty/splendor that always transcends everything we can conceive. In this "life" all properties ascribable to God are superseded: every power can be found in this beauty (Song of Songs 8:6), especially at that moment when it is disarming every worldly power by becoming so nakedly and powerlessly exposed to it. Every wisdom can be seen here, especially at the moment when it behaves as folly to every worldly wisdom. All lordship over Being is located here, precisely when it has chosen for itself something nonexistent for its appearing in order to prove that what exists is as nothing in relation to God.

c. If the hypostasis of the Son has taken on human form in order to reveal this absolute love as "Word" (showing, saying, and giving), then this "Word" speaks of nothing else but the tri-une love of God, in teaching, in life and Cross, in judging everything that is not love. This is a Word that proves itself to be the work of love. Now we see: if Jesus characterizes himself as Truth, he does so because he reveals this triune love in his whole existence and mediates it in the Holy Spirit, and he reaches this culmination of his work when he has allowed every form of sinful non-love to vent itself on him. And by taking on everything that rebels against God, he buries it in death and the grave.

But such statements seem to forget the main problem: How can the Absolute make itself present, definitively, in an ephemeral, finite life form? From the world's perspective, this seems impossible. But who can say it is a priori impossible for God simply because it contains an inherent impossibility? We can discern two approaches to this "possibility". The first moves with the argument of the opening of the Letter to the Hebrews: "In many and various ways God spoke of old to our fathers by the prophets", but he has now spoken to us uniquely "by a Son, whom he appointed the heir of all things" (Heb 1:1–2). But even in these "various times" and "various ways" God has spoken *in his unity*. As we have more extensively shown in *The Glory of the Lord* (volume 7), this means that he has united in himself, not paradoxically or dialectically, but effortlessly and as a total pattern [*gestalthaft*] what could not be united "in past times": the High Priest and the slain Lamb, the King and the Servant, the Temple and the worshipper inside the Temple, the sacred and the profane, and finally his origin in God and his birth as man. And he does this, when all is said and done, not by shattering the old tablets of the Law, but by "fulfil[ling] the scripture" (Jn 19:28).

But this is not enough: he represents within the world absolute love by once more effortlessly and undialectically unifying in his person the forms of love that seem to us in the world so contrary: he brings into himself the peace and the reconciliation of those who are hostile to him (Eph 2:14ff.), but he is simultaneously both the sword of decision that divides men as well as the sword of persecution. He demands service and worship for God alone, but at the same time he fuses this demand to a command to serve the neighbor who is in need, so that both demands completely coincide. He maintains he has come into the world not to judge but to save, and yet at the same time the whole judgment has been handed over to him. He says he has conquered the whole world through his existence and has expelled the ruler of this world, so hostile to God, but yet he still must struggle on through all of world history until he has overcome all rebellious powers (1 Cor 15:25; Rev 17:14). These apparent contradictions are already transcended and reconciled in his form; and both sides of an otherwise irresolvable dilemma, which remain tensions in other religions, are in him one, without violence.

Needless to say, this unity cannot be constructed on the basis of man's constitution but can appear as a credible unity only when God reveals himself as love; and on that basis we can lead a truly human existence, in believing discipleship. All attempts to explain this union of opposites that works from below from a purely human perspective will run aground on the reef of our finitude, because we can only depict in our minds individual moments in the figure of Christ by ignoring the others.

The most simplistic version of this strategy is the attempt to represent the original synthesis as a subsequent work of the early Church. The argument is familiar and claims that the Old Testament and Hellenistic titles were only later applied to Jesus (a thesis that would rob the *argumentum ex prophetia* of its cogency); the "I am" statements that ascribe to him a divine dignity are, accordingly, later accretions built up as occlusions from statements that were originally merely ordinary statements about his self, while his demand for humility and service can be reduced to a purely human ethic. And so (and this is the ultimate assessment of Jesus for Judaism and Islam) he is one of the prophets, which is also what the people took him to be (Lk 9:19).

But all these attempts to burst the figural unity of Jesus, where a believer finds no kind of contradiction whatever, not only make this unity humanly incredible but also destroy, above all (as the First Letter of John repeatedly stresses), the sentence that supports the whole of the Christian message: "God is love." "Every spirit that dissolveth (*luei*) Jesus is not of God" (1 Jn 4:3, Vulgate [Douay-Rheims]). The evangelists themselves confess that the indissoluble unity of the figure of Jesus as the revelation of absolute love is definitively "decipherable" only from Jesus' freely assumed death on the Cross.

But one cannot say that the absolutely incomprehensible reality that "God is love" has become graspable in the form of Christ, for it is without analogy. This would be an outright contradiction. Christ's form is no statically placed memorial but is entirely to be understood as something that points beyond itself. The Cross says: "This is how much God has loved the world" (see Jn 3:16). And which God is that? God the Father, whose Word to the world is Jesus' own word, in whose love the Father's love is to be "interpreted" (see Jn 1:18). And it is God the Spirit, the Spirit of love, who is continually explaining this Word of immeasurable love for us and in us. The word in Scripture: "No one has ever seen God" and the second half of that verse: "The only begotten God who dwells in the bosom of the Father has made him known" do not contradict each other: the second does not supersede or abolish the first but confirms it, by interpreting it.

Here, finally, it becomes clear why it is crucial to stress "simplicity of sight" (Mt 6:22; Lk 11:34) so much when we encounter the form of Jesus. The Greek word for the simple people, *haplous*, means here both "lacking convolutions" and "healthy".[1] For only the healthy/simple eye can see together the apparent contrasts in the figure of Jesus in their unity, only the *nēpioi*, the little ones, the poor, the uneducated, are not seduced by an ever-increasing accumulation of nuggets of knowledge to consider individual traits only for themselves, thereby missing the figure because they are lost in pure analysis.

But this negative of not being educated works here as a positive; not as an achievement wrestled for and won by the simple person himself, but as that lack that suits the "good pleasure" of God, that is, of the Father (Mt 11:25–28), who has revealed

[1] For further theological reflections on this theme, see *Christen sind einfältig* (1983), *Convergences*, trans. E. A. Nelson (San Francisco: Ignatius Press, 1983), and "The Faith of the Simple Ones", in *Explorations in Theology*, III: *Creator Spirit*, trans. Brian McNeil (San Francisco: Ignatius Press, 1993), 57–83.

himself in his Son. It also suits the "good pleasure" of the Son (Mt 11:27), whose one desire is to reveal. What is revealed is precisely the mutual, exclusive knowledge between Father and Son. This is a knowledge in which no one achieves insight without revelation, whose free and gracious radiation, however, only becomes effective to the one whose vision is simple. In the figure of Jesus, the "super-essential" [*hyperousion*] mystery of triune love becomes evident, both on the basis of this figure's constitution as well as because of the radiating grace that it in turn radiates outward.

This does not mean that poor simplicity can strike up an attitude of indifference, turning toward or away from God as it chooses. The denuding, the poverty (of the *anawim*) is meant only to point to God alone (only the "poor in spirit" are called blessed). True poverty of spirit does not trust in itself, as if it were some postulate, but wishes only that the grace of God's good pleasure direct the soul.

The ability to see the mystery of God's love with the simple eye is not due alone to the good will of the triune God as such. True spiritual insight occurs most especially because of a readiness on the part of the eye that by divine grace has willingly let itself be impoverished and made simple. But, in the final analysis, the simplicity of the human eye and of the spirit is the only truly appropriate organ for receiving that self-presentation of God in Christ, who has characterized himself as "meek and gentle of heart" and who has invited us to accept this, his existential teaching, because it is precisely with the same attitude that he has revealed most clearly the mystery of triune love.

If we want to speak of meditation and the plunge into the depths of divine revelation, then this cannot happen without the accent falling on the Incarnation of the Son, a reality we can never transcend or move beyond. Only through this "shining forth" does the central statement that God is love evade the delimiting habits of human measurement. But if we try to get around or beyond God's epiphany, he becomes the abyss, the hollow—the One, the Absolute Being. Above all, we must not overlook that everything in Christ—the circumincession in him of all transcendentals, even in their intraworldly polarity—always remains a pointer to God's wealth of love, because he is the Word of the Father in the Spirit in such a way that the transcendentals appearing in him, as we have shown, are the revelation of the tri-personal vitality of God. If this a posteriori reference were everything, then the contemplative person at prayer would be justifiably inclined to try to strive to get away from the revealer merely to what was being revealed. But as John's theology warns us, there is the opposite pointer of the Father to the Son, past whom we can never reach the Father. "This is my beloved Son; listen to him"—whether that hearkening means seeing or believing, experiencing or not experiencing. The one at prayer, persevering simultaneously in both movements, can be sure of persevering in the Holy Spirit, who unites both.

2

THE WORD BECOMES FLESH

a. Entry into the inner sanctum remains essentially a step unacceptable to pagan, Jew, and Moslem. All of them reject the assertion *Verbum caro factum est*. For them the Word of God can only be a prophetic word, but never God himself, nor can God *become* something he has not previously always been. But the Christian religion emphatically maintains: the Word both was "with God" as well as being itself "God", and, moreover, *became* something. So crucial is this doctrine that God could actually "become" (turn into) something else that Christianity goes to the fullest extremes in stressing this: not merely did God become "man", but he became *flesh* (*caro*, *sarx*, which of course means "man" here, since by that term the Old Testament always meant the concrete, temporal, and frail human animal). By using this term Christianity puts man's frailty, vulnerability, and, above all, his mortality at the very center of the doctrine of the Incarnation. This focus on the body as the locus of salvation (*caro cardo salutis* goes the patristic axiom: "the flesh is the hinge of salvation") represents the kernel of truth in the early Christian Logos-Sarx Christology, until it grew to an exaggerated and heretical form with Apollinaris, who claimed that the Logos replaced the human mind of Jesus, which made the term "flesh" refer only to the physical body of Jesus. This extreme extrapolation had to be rectified later, but the later heretical conclusion drawn from the premises of Logos-Sarx Christology do not invalidate its central insight, an assertion that it shares with the whole of anti-gnostic theology, one that remains still timely for us today when so many crave to spiritualize the Christ-event—a perennial temptation for theology in every age.

The human *spirit*, however, stands in the midpoint for philosophy and every extra-biblical theology, for their habit is to set man apart from all other beings. But man still belongs to and is rooted in the world of other finite beings. He has a body that will inevitably perish; he is vulnerable to suffering and will someday "return to dust"—lowly and disquieting facts of human life that scarcely ever interest philosophy and facts that religions continually try to thwart by absorbing them into something higher, or even by trying to get around them altogether.

Of course, there is another option too: one can make suffering heroic, the way myths and tragedy do and as Nietzsche in his own way tried to replicate. But the suffering Christ has nothing in common with a hero. The hero demonstrates to us that he can "cope with" even the worst of fates. But Christ's suffering is something much more willingly embraced out of loving obedience to God's loving will, even if he takes on this destiny in fear (Lk 12:50; 22:30ff.). His plea to be released from this burden is thoroughly human (see 2 Cor 12:8). But beyond this plea, his one real urge is to persevere through his suffering by surrendering himself to God's will, something that is possible to him only because God strengthens him in his human powerlessness (Lk 22:43): the angel comes to strengthen him in his Passion solely so that he might be able to endure his weakness to the point of dying for us.

This Passion that Jesus lives for is in two respects a mystery of the body. First of all, suffering of soul in the human sense is possible only because of our bodiliness. Even if this pain has purely mental causes, it is still provoked by the body: the way we understand suffering recognizes that spiritual suffering is made possible precisely because the soul is thoroughly and completely entissued [*Eingesenktheit*] in the body. (We can discern something analogous in the phenomenon of sexuality: it certainly has its origins in bodiliness, but it makes its effects felt in all the corners of the spirit. Even in eternal life, where there will no longer be sexual procreation, a man who dies, a woman who dies, will not lose sexual identity or exchange it for something else.)

That is why we can speak only analogously when we talk about the suffering of God or the suffering of pure spirits. An angel is unable to experience abandonment by God as Jesus did on the Cross. Only Jesus could experience this as the overflowing crescendo of his rejection by the world. This is intimately connected with the second feature: world-redemptive suffering was possible only within Jesus' species-commonality with the rest of mankind, an inherent implication of his having a real, physical human body. The Greek Church Fathers clearly saw this in their theology of the Incarnation—which must not be set apart from their theology of the Cross.

The Incarnation of the Logos affects the whole of human nature because we are a totality of individuals who are established in material unity. We are certainly spiritual insofar as we are subjects immediately drawn to God, but we form a species by our common rootedness in the flesh, our fleshly emergence from one another. This is an essential presupposition for someone being able to suffer vicariously for mankind as a whole. (Here, by the way, we are discussing merely a condition for the mystery of substitution, not the mystery itself.) Saint Thomas is therefore right when he ascribes to every angel a unique species, which simultaneously excludes a natural procreation of angels but also (assuming it were meaningful to talk in this way, which it is not) vicarious suffering on their behalf.

b. Proceeding from the assertions of the prologue of John's Gospel, we must now go farther and relate not only a physically united humanity but also—even if in a different way—the material cosmos as a whole to the Incarnation of the Logos; and we must do this both protologically as well as eschatologically. The New Testament hymns in the first chapters of the Gospel of John and the Letters to the Ephesians and Colossians all agree that the cosmos as a whole, heaven and earth ("heaven" meaning the world of the stars and sky, as in Genesis), was created by the Logos (in consort with God). Crucially, however, by Logos is meant in these hymns, not some fleshless Word (*logos asarkos*), but the very Son of God who from all eternity was destined to become incarnate. "Without him nothing was made that was made." "Everything has its being in him." This originally all-creating Word will also be, "in the fullness of time", the "Savior of all", since God's plan consists in directing the course of historical time, as controlled by him, toward the Incarnation—all so that "the universe may come together under one Head in Christ, everything in the heavens and on the earth."

That protology leads to this conclusion from the outset is also shown in the eager longing of creation as depicted in Romans 8: creation "waits with eager longing", "groaning in travail"— not for the specific Incarnation of Jesus, but for its fulfillment in his Mystical Body. For we Christians, who as members of this body have already received the "warrant of the Spirit", "groan inwardly as we wait for adoption as sons, the redemption of our bodies". In no way is it the desire of creation to be spiritualized; nor do we want to live in our bodies alone—rather, we wish to be fully conformed to the Son and to his risen, spiritual body.

In both directions, from the initial creation as well as from the final redemption, the embodiment of the Logos stands at the midpoint. And because the whole of the cosmos is indivisible from man, and because man himself emerged and developed from that same cosmos and is meant to rule over it as if it were but his own body writ large, the lordship of the enfleshed Son necessarily becomes lordship over the universe. Paul's clearly marked distinction between the Church (and humanity) as "Body of Christ" and Christ's lordship over the universe in his Letters to the Ephesians and Colossians can only be understood in a mutual relation of both polarities: "In the Lord of the Church rules as well the Lord of the principalities and powers; and in the Lord of the principalities and powers the world beholds as well the Lord of the Church" so that "the drawing of the universe into the fullness (*pleroma*) can only happen through the Church and, in her, through the individual" (Schlier).

When we realize how the cosmos is being drawn into the redemption of mankind, we will see the weight and importance of the body all the more clearly, for man owes his existence as a bodily being to the cosmos and its infinite levels. Even on the bodily level of our fellow humanity with one another, there is a natural faculty for being present to one another. Indeed, this is a distant premonition and foreshadowing of the vicarious representation for all of us, brought about by Jesus by virtue of his Incarnation, a representation only God can accomplish in a human nature.

What, then, is this whole climb through millions of years of "nature" supposed to mean? For we should recall that this is a nature that could only develop because every living thing (however well equipped with defensive shells or other evolutionary mechanisms for self-defense) must necessarily offer itself to the sustenance of other "higher" creatures. And, on that allegedly higher level, what is the unspeakable history of mankind's butchery also supposed to mean? (Hans André speaks of "nature's great sacrificial triumphal march.") What can we say about human history, this grinding, pulverizing witches' millhouse of blood and tears, unless all these baffled, uncomprehending, and stunned victims finally come before God, embedded inside a final, conscious, and all-encompassing Victim? Not as if they come before a perverse tyrant, but before him who is in himself absolute surrender, who indeed is surrender beyond all imaginable forms of recklessness and who reveals this on the summit of the world!

c. My body is an incomprehensible intermediate zone between me and the world. It does not belong to me like some other object but "as if it were a piece of me"—yet it is still something like a piece of the external world. Examples like amputation continually remind me of that ineluctable fact. Yes, my body belongs to me, but it is still that item in the world through which I (often in unhealthy ways) am always bumping up against other bodies. Only so do I become aware that the world and the others, in their free independence and otherness, cannot be dominated by me for the benefit of my spirit:

> Lightly dwell thoughts alongside one another;
> But things—how hard they do collide in space![1]

If I bump up against a fellow human being, I discover two things especially: the border of my freedom and the reality of his freedom, for his freedom only becomes real to me when two bodies encounter each other. And precisely because I can experience this reality as real, I realize that I cannot do anything about it. It is simply true, and I am forced to let it be true; and only because of this hard experience of the not-I can human community arise. This collision reveals the juxtaposition of freedoms

---

[1] "Leicht beieinander wohnen die Gedanken, / Doch hart im Raume stoßen sich die Sachen."

that become present to each other, and so collision of freedoms becomes the presupposition for life together. The German for "presence" [*Gegenwart*, rooted in *wärtig*, itself rooted in the Latin *vertere*, "to turn"] literally means to be turned toward another.

Only when we discover the mystery of the other, as mediated by the body, can true community arise. And therefore community can never be organized from some neutral height (sociologically or politically) without eventually turning the person into a number and without the living individual body becoming a piece of manipulable matter. But where the clash of bodies is transformed into a mutual facing of one another—and it will do so because the physical senses are the occasion for mutual cognition and recognition—there and only there will there arise that "between word"—or as we say, following the Greek term, "dia-logue".

This preliminary reflection was needed so that we could understand the meaning of incarnation. In the man Jesus we encounter an other so strange that at first we cannot manage to pigeonhole him in any known category of fellow human being. "Who do people say that I am?" Well, perhaps a prophet, preferably one of the older ones we already know—Jeremiah, Elijah. . . . But the categories break down. "Who do *you* say that I am?" Let us leave it undecided at the moment what Peter might have meant in his own mind when he used terms like "Messiah" and "Son of God". In any case, as the rest of the story shows ("The Son of Man must suffer"), it was not an adequate answer.

But think of how infinitely difficult it would have been to guess that the personal Word of *God himself* was speaking out of this man, who was so obviously and so bodily present to them! This would mean that everything we discussed in the middle part of this *Epilogue* (that the All-Real was expressing itself, giving itself, enunciating itself) was now supposed to be happening *right here*, right inside the course of world history, in the encounter of living bodies!

In everything that had previously happened in history—in the covenant between God and man, in the law, in the prophetic word, in the cultic sacrifice—something like a dialogue was initiated. But a *definitive* self-showing, self-saying, self-giving had not taken place. For that, something else would have been necessary, which we have already met in the line cited from the poem above: "But things: how hard they do collide in space!" And yet for those who felt the impact of this collision, this would have still been preposterous, inconceivable: for God is in his heaven, and we are on earth, since God of course is spirit, and we are bodies. Or if he were to be a body, certainly it would not be this individual and mortal body, so comparable to all other *corpora*. A thing that one can touch with one's senses: impossible that this *thing* is the one, all-encompassing God!

John begins his great First Epistle by leading off with a bold assertion of this absolute scandal: "What we have seen, heard, and touched with our hands is the Word of eternal life." He heightens the scandal further throughout his writings; but at the same time he points out how it has been overcome, in a way we cannot understand, when he has Jesus say in his discourse on the Eucharist in the sixth chapter of his Gospel after the multiplication of the loaves: "My body is real food and my blood is real drink." Note how the people of Capernaum understood this saying as a kind of cannibalism—but then, who could understand it in any other way if he stopped to think about it? Such a claim was intolerable and abominable!

Whereupon Jesus told his disciples that they could leave him, too, if they felt that this teaching of his was the breaking point of their faith in him. After such a challenge, all the disciples could do was to trust him, blindly and helplessly: "Where can we go, since you have the words of eternal life?" But how could his assertion be imagined? How could the reality of this body—a reality that could not be abolished if Jesus as the one who "has made [God] known" (Jn 1:18) was not to be rendered invalid—be united with the abolition of the limits set to material bodies?

Even after the Resurrection, when the disciples were directly faced with precisely this suspension of the limits of the body, faith was difficult: a body that went in and out through closed doors yet could still be touched! "A spirit does not have flesh and bone as you see in me. Do you have something here to eat?" Doubting Thomas represents the dilemma of all of us: faith must trump sight once more, indeed, in this case definitively.

Otherwise there is no access to the central mystery of the Eucharist, in which finally the most contrary polarities converge: (1) true body and true blood, in which God shows, gives, and speaks himself; and (2) the structure of definitive human community, in which the individual self-presenting bodies become temples of the Holy Spirit of Christ; but in his own body they are also but *one* temple.

Fleshly, earthly thought (*kata sarka*) must be stunned in the face of an ultimate "spiritual understanding of the body", what Paul calls the *sōma pneumatikon*, but that is the only understanding that will lead us to Christ's eucharistic Body, distributed throughout the world. And we should not fancy that words like flesh and blood hold true only up to the Resurrection, even if we cannot imagine how a transfigured body is still to contain something that we normally understand by *blood*. Yet we should consider: from the very beginning blood has been *the* life element in man belonging to God (Gen 9:4–6). The central vision of Catherine of Siena, now officially proclaimed a Doctor of the Church, was that of the Blood of Christ continually circulating to give life and purification in the Church and mankind. (Unfortunately, the limitations of this *Epilogue* do not allow us to examine the issues raised by the many miracles of blood.)

The words of institution also gain their meaning and power after Easter. "This is a hard saying; who can listen to it?" (Jn 6:60). So it is. But it cannot be said in any other way if the body really is to be the natural interpretation or symbol of the spirit, if God wants to meet us in a way appropriate to his own creation according to its own forms of interpretation, if he wants to enter into community with us: God's epiphany is manifest in Jesus Christ ("No one knows the Father except the Son and those to whom the Son wishes to reveal him"). God gives himself to us in Christ and expresses himself to us in him. But to understand this completely in faith means that we will also have to accept the other hard word, that of vicarious representation.

d. Faith in the "resurrection" of the flesh of Christ and then of all "those who belong to Christ" (1 Cor 15:21–23) only intensifies the realization that man, as a physical, biological being of nature and, like all other subhuman members of the natural order, is a "being headed toward death". This gives to him and his bodily works and encounters their enduring value but also their sadness. Gilgamesh's search for immortality was in vain; and Euridice could not be brought back from Hades. All religions outside the Old Testament were and are attempts to flee this tragedy. This is especially true in the assertion of the immortality of the soul, a soul that flees the prison of the world. That is why the Old Testament knows so well the demand for a long life, necessarily understood as God's blessing. Israel did not know of an underworld mythology the way the Egyptians and most of the surrounding peoples did. Israel was being prepared by God for the only possible solution to human tragedy: the Resurrection of God's Son from the dead, the bursting open of the gates of Sheol.

A complete transvaluation of death and its empire follows and, from this, a transvaluation of human existence [*Dasein*] as "being headed toward death". For the death of Christ in God's plan of salvation is the perfecting highpoint of his love shown to the world. In the Incarnation of the eternal Son, death is already taken up as the expression of God's love for the creature, especially the sinner. Death *as* love is a thought imaginable within the Old Covenant. As with all peoples, there is the death of the hero (David praises Saul and Jonathan as just such heroes in his funeral lament for them); there is the death of martyrs (the brothers Maccabee); there is the contrast of the strength of love with the strength of death (Song 8:6). But that the notion of death as such—indeed, dying in the frightful darkness that the psalms associate with the essence of death and the realm of the dead—could be interpreted as the highest love directly contradicts Israel's entire understanding of the covenant.

That is why Jesus was met with complete misunderstanding by his disciples when he foretold so contemptible a death for himself. And when death came, it contained all the somber colors from the psalms, fragments of which he speaks on the Cross and whose statements he could rightly appropriate to himself. But to understand this horror as the work of highest love was reserved for him alone. After him those who believe in him can adopt such an understanding of death. Henceforward, dying can now be seen—beyond being our naturally constrained end—to be the perfect surrender of oneself into the hands of the Father; death is now an opportunity for letting everything go and being free in God. The highest work of the body is brought to perfection here, its ultimate dignity revealed. This dignity transcends the body's physical finitude and has—as the expression of infinite love—a claim to share in God's eternal life. And not only as a living body but precisely as a body that has died. This transvaluation of death in the greatest act of life perfectly reveals that death, as the total surrender to God, is co-transformed in the "spiritual body" over which "death no longer has dominion" (Rom 6:9) because its has been "swallowed up" (1 Cor 15:54) in God's own vitality.

3

FRUITFULNESS

a. In our discussion of the transcendentals, the deepest mystery of Being came into view only imperfectly. All beings essentially and increasingly appear as epiphanic: they are all inherently self-showing, self-giving, and self-expressing. And all three modes, each drawing in and including the other two, emerge as essential features of the act of being. But this aspect of self-openness is also endowed with the miracle of fruitfulness, at least where we are speaking of living beings (ignoring for the moment prime matter, before it receives the forms). Already in the account of creation, the plants are to bear fruit, fruit that contains in itself new seed (Gen 1:11). The animals are to be fruitful and increase and multiply (1:22), and the same for man (1:28).

That this faculty for procreation and giving birth is connected with the finitude and death of these beings is not explicitly mentioned in Genesis, but the connection becomes all too obvious to anyone who thinks about the evolution of the cosmos. But even when we make explicit in our minds the connection between fruitfulness and death, the former still remains the inconceivable miracle of the living. Because this miracle is innately bound to the hylomorphic composition of the body (angels cannot procreate), we must distinguish two features here: first, that the transcendentals (taken as a unity) allow beings to strive beyond themselves: *surrender creates new beings*; secondly, that a moment of death always lies in this surrender (as Hegel stressed): as if in anticipation of the ultimate supernatural surrender of Christ ("in whom all things have their being") in the purely everyday phenomena of nature, as explained above. There are animals who die in the ecstasy of copulation (others survive, but, as it were, only to rear their offspring and make them capable of living), so that their own dissolution is one with the growth in vitality of others who owe their existence to their dying progenitors.

It was above all the task of the third part of the trilogy, the *Theo-Logic*, to show in detail how the miracle of cosmic fertility is the stamp and image of the original mystery of Being as such, of its trinitarian constitution; and it has already been mentioned here, too. But if this prior mystery in Jesus Christ expresses and bestows itself in the language of the world, and if in this language death gains an entirely new meaning, then the expression of absolute triune fruitfulness must also step out of the natural cycle of procreation and death and assume another, but no less bodily, form: a form in which dying (as in the archetype of the Cross) coincides with the highest fruitfulness of life, which no longer generates anything mortal but rather something that already belongs to the eternal, triune-fruitful life of God. "There are eunuchs who have made themselves eunuchs for the sake of the kingdom of heaven" (Mt 19:12).

This holds true in a spiritual sense for all Christians (1 Cor 7:29). But for those "who can grasp it", those to whom "it has been given to know the secrets of the kingdom of heaven" (Mt 13:11), it is also true in a literal sense. Since even those who renounce marriage for the kingdom do so in order to follow the incarnate Word, we are obviously not talking about any downplaying of the flesh or of the Incarnation here. On the contrary, their surrender of their bodies is now for the sake of a new fruitfulness, one that is not only spiritual but, following the example of Christ, also physical.

Recall the Old Testament anticipations: whenever the fruitfulness of the line of God's promises of salvation is at stake, it is always God who assists the withered fruitfulness of the man and woman, and thus it is *God* who becomes the primary model of fertility: as we see in the example of Abraham and Sarah, Hannah as well, and with a special radiance in the example of Zechariah and Elizabeth.

Here is where refulgent light falls on Joseph: at this point in salvation history the divine fruitfulness possesses such a preponderance over the purely sexual fertility of man that natural fertility can now concede the whole place to God's fruitfulness. This now becomes possible because with Jesus the worldly cycle of (natural) reproduction following fast and inevitably on (natural) death has been definitively broken, and this enables his death to be the highest expression of life and love. So Joseph, when he

renounces human fertility, takes his place among those named in
Matthew 19:12: his virginal fruitfulness cannot be divided from
that of his spouse, Mary.

But whereas the supernatural fruitfulness of the marriage between Joseph and Mary forms the perfect conclusion to a series
of marriages beginning with that between Abraham and Sarah
(a series that of course remains fruitful in all subsequent history), Jesus' gift of Mary the "woman" and John the "son" to
each other becomes the prelude to the fruitfulness established
for his Church by the crucified Lord. Mary, the Mother of Jesus
(whom he always addresses as "woman" in John) becomes the
"spouse" of the "new Adam", of the "Lamb", in her sharing in
the suffering of the Cross. She receives the Beloved Disciple as
her son, who is as virginal as she but who is also one of the apostles, through whose mediation she is inducted into the apostolic
Church.

This giving away of a man and a woman from the Cross shows
—even when this action transcends the natural-sexual sphere (for
they are of course mother and son)—the lasting importance of
sexual difference within the Church of Christ. This becomes
clear in a number of ways. When Mary is told that she is now
no longer to consider her physical Son, but the Beloved Disciple,
to be "her son", we recall the imperishable fruitfulness of her
virginal motherhood, meant for us all and for herself. But since
this son is a man like Jesus (who, on the Cross, as we recall,
addressed Mary as "woman"), a substitution takes place. This
admonishes both the Mother and John not to overlook their
sexual difference and permits their union to appear as the real
symbol for the fruitfulness of the crucified man Jesus.

And right at this moment there emerges a third motif, apparently at cross-purposes with the other two: when Paul draws
the parallels between the way Eve came from Adam and the
way the Church springs forth from Christ (Eph 5)—which is
even more underlined in John in his portrayal of the way the substance of the Church flowed out from the wounded side of Jesus
—the man Jesus becomes the origin of the woman and spouse
Church in the fruitfulness of his death, so that the virginity of
Mary (*and* the virginity of John, too, who, needless to say, is a

member of the Church) are both finally derived from that of her physical Son. Thus is fulfilled at the highest level what Paul says: "As woman [first] was made from man, so man is now born of woman. And all things are from God" (1 Cor 11:12).

Two aspects of the supra-sexual and virginal fruitfulness are thus inseparably woven together: a personal aspect (that of Mary and John) and a sacramental one (blood and water and, accompanying this, the outpouring of the Spirit [Jn 19:30]), which, however, just like the first aspect is not impersonal but stems from the personal, dying body of Christ.

We must now specify this more exactly from the perspective of Christ's identity as *Verbum-Caro*. His mission from the Father is universal, but it goes out from him as a particular human being. He himself becomes universal by virtue of his death, in which he opens up the innermost depths of his body and surrenders his Spirit without ceasing to be the particular and unique being that he is. Here we clearly see that his universalization (as always, this could be more exactly understood) must contain within itself both moments of his fruitfulness. First, his universal presence as Lord must be something bodily; it must be something over which he governs but which is not in that way identical with him: the new Eve, the Church, arose from this body, but as his Bride. Second, the Church's universality (corresponding to his) must be a mission to all peoples as the sacrament for the salvation of the world.

To put this more exactly: the incarnate Word is both the epiphany as well as the self-bestowal and self-expression of God, and this applies to all of Jesus' existence as a being of body and soul. We may treat this under three rubrics, aspects that the Gospel narratives stress more and more sharply: (1) his epiphany of God (under this rubric the Church as a social incorporation will be his bodily re-presentation in the world and for it); (2) there is his self-surrender (in this aspect the Church will understand herself both as his "Body" as well as his "Bride" before the world and to herself); and (3) finally, there is God expressing himself in him (under this rubric we say the Church owes her existence to his oral commission: "Do this", "Go forth to teach and baptize", "As the Father sent me, so I send you", and so

forth). Considered from the point of view of Jesus' identity as
the incarnate Word and reflecting on his fruitfulness that follows
from this, we see that these aspects of the Church that we have
enumerated here can be separated from one another just as little
as the transcendentals could be unwoven and then divided into
sharply demarcated categories.

Finally we should consider the way Jesus shared in our humanity by virtue of his being *Verbum caro factum*. As a fellow human
being with us, Jesus can do no other than draw other human
beings into his unique and incomparable work. And so he calls
others to join with him in the special task of continuing his work.
From the very beginning, in the call of the Twelve, Jesus gave a
share in his authority both before the Passion ("Do this") and
after it ("Whose sins you shall forgive . . ."), drawing them ever
more deeply into his own mission. In this way he made them
capable as well of drawing others into his special mission. We
must see all these aspects together, as intimately bound up with
each other, if we want to perceive, at least to some extent, the
mystery of the fruitfulness of the continued life of the incarnate
Word—called the Church—without abridgment.

b. If we now want to proceed from here and speak of the Church
as sacrament and of her individual sacraments, then we will still
have to return to the Body of Christ. According to Hebrews
10:6, Christ said upon coming into the world: "Sacrifices and
offerings you have not desired, but a body have you prepared
for me. . . . Behold, I am come to do your will" (quoting Psalm
40:7–8, according to the Septuagint translation). The body re-
ferred to here means the presentation of the "I" in the visible
field of the world. But this body is also the appropriate replace-
ment for the purely external sacrifices and offerings and, simultaneously, the realization for the inner will to fulfill the divine
will. If Christ is the originating sacrament as appearance, surrender, and expression of God's love for the world, then by means
of the eucharistic universalizing of this personally surrendered
body, the Church receives a share in this original sacramentality.
Moreover, the Church shares this reality by drawing the faithful
into his "life-creating spirit [body]" (1 Cor 15:45; or "Mystical

Body") as well as by being the "Bride" who is "one flesh" (Eph 5:31) with him and who comes forth from him, for she is the fruit of his sacrificed body.

In both these aspects the Church owes her fruitfulness to the sacrifice of Christ's body; this is why she is forbidden to fall into the temptation of equating her primal sacramental character with his. Nor, on the other hand, may we sunder these two initial levels from one another, severing the bodily emergence of the Church from the sacrificial body of Christ. It is from this reality that the incarnate Word first calls the Twelve (as foundation stones of the Church [Rev 21:14]) and increasingly equips them with his authority. The Church is not there first as mere institution that then subsequently (on the Cross) receives its life principle through blood, water, and Spirit. For one thing, the sacramental bonding of the Twelve in the Last Supper, celebrated *before* the Passion yet directed to bringing them into the fruitfulness of the Cross, speaks against such dichotomizing. Secondly, this dichotomizing is contradicted by the fact that Jesus establishes the original cell of the Church in the community between Mary and John at the end of his surrender to God on the Cross, the final word before Scripture reaches its perfect fulfillment (Jn 19:26–28).

Therefore, the Church is the originating sacrament springing up from Christ's material, physical nature, and in all the aspects mentioned above. She participates in Christ's universal mission of salvation and in the power he has to effect it (in this sense, the otherwise easily misunderstood maxim is true that "outside of the Church there is no salvation"). She is, like Christ himself, a particular body with a universal mission and a universal effect for the world. For she is, considered as a unity, the Mystical Body and Bride of Christ. But this also holds true a fortiori of those members who are most intimately bonded with Christ's attitude and with his true Church.

One of the areas where the Church establishes her efficacy is in her life as it is configured by the individual sacraments radiating out from her. In these sacraments she presents in *bodily* form the decisive incorporation into Christ's and the Church's salvific efficacy for us physical beings in the most notable situations in life. The sacraments are necessarily inscribed in these natural (but also already graced) moments in life, which are already characterized in the natural plane by sacral rites: birth, puberty, marriage, festive meals, illness, death, and burial. Across all societies these are, so to speak, "natural sacraments", for the celebration of which there must also be the competent faculty and authority for presiding over these moments, which directly entails the need to set aside certain persons for the offering of sacrifices to the divinity, which in turn implies their sacral consecration to the governance of the people.

Over and above this anthropological constant, we discover another layer—the Old Testament anticipatory rites given in the reality of the covenant, the most conspicuous being: the physical rite of circumcision, the marking out of marriage as the symbol of the covenant to be established at the coming of the Messiah, along with the institution of the priesthood for the concrete reenactment of the covenant rituals.

But in the New Covenant all of this is overtaken by the underivable reality of Christ as *Verbum-Caro*. This new and utterly unexpected reality places the Eucharist in the center of sacramental reality, as the immediate incorporation into the bodily saving efficacy of Christ and Church. From this center all the other sacramental situations are related to this Body: since the Baptism of Jesus constituted his consecration for his public mission, and since he not only directed his disciples to baptize even during his earthly ministry (Jn 4:2) but also expressly instructed them to go out and baptize all nations after his Resurrection (Mt 28:19), sacramental baptism has its ultimate foundation as a form of consecration in the Baptism in the River Jordan, where the triune God confesses himself in the Sonship of Jesus and his mission.

The distinction between the sacraments of confirmation and baptism arose for two reasons: first, because of the "natural sacrament" of human maturation, but also because of the distance between Christ's own Baptism and the pouring out of the Holy

Spirit during the *Triduum Paschale* (or at Pentecost). The institution of human marriage and its fruitfulness in children is expressly placed in the context of the relations of Christ and his
Church (Eph 5). Priestly ordination has its origin in the bodily self-surrender of Jesus at the Last Supper and in his breath-
ing upon the apostles at Easter, bestowing on them the grace
to celebrate these mysteries. In spite of certain adumbrations in
the Old Testament, the forgiveness of sins has its true source
in Christ's assuming the sin of the world when he died on the
Cross, descended to the dead, and rose to new life on Easter
morning, winning thereby eternal forgiveness for the human
race. The sacrament of the anointing of the sick and Last Rites
for the dying come from Jesus' special care for the sick ("Those
who are well have no need of a physician, but those who are
sick" [Lk 5:31; see 5:17]), from his instruction to the disciples
to heal the sick by anointing them with oil (Mk 6:13); from
the execution of these instructions in the early Church (see Jas
5:14), from his assurance that he is the resurrection and the life
for mortal bodies (Jn 11:25ff.), and from his own submission
to being anointed by Mary of Bethany before his death.

Thus what happens in the seven sacraments is this: the one
who brought salvation to the world did so by living a fully human life, which means submitting himself, not just to the various
major turning points of a human life, but also to the Jewish rites
marking them out. Because he was the bearer of our salvation,
his various life situations thus touch the basic situations of human existence in such a way that the latter (whose symbolic and
sacral value every healthy culture recognizes through ritual) are
marked and grounded in the foundational events of Jesus' life,
which means all the turning points of human life in a Christian
are thereby made fruitful for generating Christ's own life in the
Church.

And just because the Eucharist steps forth as the most central of the Church's sacraments, this does not mean that the Eucharist lacks its own natural basis in human anthropology (as
we see in the parable of the wedding banquet in Matthew 22);
nor does it permit us to dispense with the Old Testament an-

ticipatory signs (like the Passover seder). But the centrality of
the Eucharist means above all that it is the seal of the definitive
Word-made-flesh. If "man lives by everything that proceeds out
of the mouth of the LORD" (Deut 8:3 = Mt 4:4; Jn 4:34), then
the words of Jesus are "spirit and life" (Jn 6:63), for the Word
has become flesh and is given for us as "food indeed" and "drink
indeed" (Jn 6:55).

So Christ dispenses himself in the sacraments within the
Church, too: "Christ is the one who baptizes through the
Church, who teaches, rules, loosens, binds, offers sacrifice and
sanctifies, enlivening his whole Body with his divine power"
(DS 3806). But Christ effects all of this with the commission
and authority of the Father through the Holy Spirit they have
in common. For that reason in all three Synoptic Gospels the
true Lord of the table in the eucharistic banquet is the heavenly
Father, who sets out for us the best he has to offer. Similarly, the
precious taste of the gifts welling up within all the sacraments
comes from the Holy Spirit, the Spirit of the giving Father and
of the Son who lets himself be given as food and drink. It is
the Spirit who enables us, when we pray the Canon of the Mass
with the Church, to address all thanks and gratitude, all honor
and glory, through him and with the Son to the Father.

c. Even with all that we have mentioned about God's fruitfulness in Christ, we have yet to touch upon the central point from
which everything radiates and converges. To be sure, we have
been circling this point, but we have not yet looked at it directly.
It lies in the very center between two secure truths, but we cannot easily see how they can be unified. On the one hand, Jesus
announces the coming reign of God; he is ready to forgive all
guilt, to fulfill the covenant by wanting to forgive and forget
all man's infidelity. And Jesus searches for people who are ready
to make this small conversion to the God of love, that almost
insignificant step, one that, to Jesus, is understood better by the
simple than by the clever and learned, by the sick better than by
the healthy, by sinners better than by the righteous.

At the other fork of the dilemma is the fact that God never

forces his love on any of the self-righteous; indeed, the brighter shines his light, the more tenacious are they entrenched in their darkness and blindness. Pure love, now become man and our closest neighbor, forces out into the open the most perverted monstrosities of sin, forcing them to expose themselves. "If I had not come and spoken to them, they would not have sin" (Jn 15:22). "If you were blind, you would have no guilt; but now that you say, 'We see,' your guilt remains" (Jn 9:41). One can indeed say that Jesus announces an unconditional forgiveness by God, but in doing so he has not said that men have accepted it. Just the opposite: only in the New Covenant is there such an absolute threat as that against the pharisaical hypocrites (Mt 23) or against the unbelieving cities (Mt 11:20–24). Conversion is not something we can promise to do; it must actually be accomplished.

We have now come to the point where we must inquire how the mystery of the Cross should be seen as an *admirabile commercium* (a wondrous exchange of places). It would be infantile to interpret this exchange of places theatrically, that is, to expect that Jesus could have put on some kind of didactic play in his public ministry (although some theologians seem to regret this). Such an expectation would represent a total misunderstanding of the tragedy of Jesus (and woe unto us, says Reinhold Schneider, if we deny the tragic in Christ's life and in Christianity at large, which consists precisely in this: that the ever-greater weight of the proof of God's love always highlights the ever-increasing hatred for God). If we try to argue that God the Father wanted to prove to us in Jesus' journey to the Cross how much he loves the world (by the way: how comical for a God to have to prove *that* to us!), that still does nothing to address the contingency of someone turning away from God in hate.

The same would hold true if we simply wanted to say that Jesus had remained true to his "solidarity" with sinners to the very end. What is the point of such garish testimonials to love? Scratch the surface of that logic, and soon the only response will turn out to be: to turn away in contempt. And that response will become all the more inevitable when men hear theologians assuring us that God is nothing else but love, and all this talk about God's "wrath" (think of René Girard and his epigones) is but a false transposition of human emotions onto God.

But this is to judge God, not to let God judge us through the Cross. The difficult question thus lies, not on God's side, but on man's rejection of God. Here is the rub: How can the fact that a man who was born and lived in a backwater corner of the Roman Empire and was crucified two thousand years ago (with countless thousands of others, by the way), and this out of love for me, motivate me to change my life? By touching me with a love that no one can prove to me is love? By letting an automaton play a part here? But then what would become of my freedom? I could never let myself be deceived in this way. It would be like taking one of those truth serums used in the interrogation techniques of totalitarian countries. One speaks constantly of "vicarious representation". But please, this is valid only if I see the sense of it. But just think of what this really is supposed to mean: First, I find myself declared guilty of I know not what, like some character out of a Kafka novel, and then I am told that someone has just taken my place in prison. And I am supposed to believe both these assertions!

So obviously we will have to proceed cautiously with this term "vicarious representation". Jesus can hardly push the sinner aside to make room for his own place. He cannot appropriate for himself the sinner's freedom to do with it what the sinner did not himself want to do. Even more pointedly: he can "redeem" me (the word "redemption" refers primarily to ransom paid to release someone from prison, slavery, or debt), but never without my permission: I must continually *accept* this deed, letting it be true for me. Free men are not pieces of luggage, after all, that can be "redeemed" from the lost and found.

We are clearly entangled in the thickest knots of a mystery that can only be unraveled with great care. Let us distinguish four key features that are entailed in the concept of "redemption".

First, it refers to the status and commission of the Son of God. According to the Cyrillian and Chalcedonian view of human nature, Jesus holds a position that alters the whole of this nature (as we say: for he shares in the materiality of all other humans). According to his dignity, he is the Head who makes all others the members, although we have yet to determine exactly how. Let us assume that the whole of this nature finds itself to be in an explicitly negative place before God; then Jesus will appropriate to himself this negative position—in accord with his commission and his inner ability and freedom—in such a way that it will be transformed by him into what it is in truth: into the pain of alienation that now is experienced no longer simply by God but by man, too. (Recall here that we are discussing this issue on the plane of the total structure of divine versus human nature; the question of individual freedom has not yet been mooted.)

But second, we should admit that the change effected by the Head of the human race is realized only from this position, that is, as from someplace "above" the totality of human nature. And this change transforms the situatedness of all who belong to this nature with their personal freedom. We should recall here something said earlier: the Incarnation and the Cross have their "place" where the *actus completus non subsistens* is at work in created reality, which is realized only in individual beings. The Son of God in no way replaces this act. But if "everything in heaven and on earth has its being in him", then he is the head of everything that has been created from that identity. And the free assumption not only of human nature but also of its alienation can thus ensue only "above" or "beyond" or "beneath" the situatedness of all natural beings.

At the same time Incarnation means that the assumption of human nature, along with all its attendant forms of alienation, surpasses this nature and its alienations for something infinite. This is because, to put it bluntly, no one can be abandoned by the Father as the Son was, who is the only one who knows the Father as he really is (Mt 11:27). Thus our attempt to illuminate this mystery has moved forward by a step, an essential step in fact, without, of course, our having yet addressed the question of the relationship between "redemption" and the "individual will".

Something else as well that until now has not been considered can now be explained: the dialectical relationship between Cross and Eucharist. The expressions "given up for us" and "poured out for us" are no mere phrases but are pure reality: our situation before God, as sinners, has been transformed by Jesus into his own position before God, and he gives back to us what once was ours and now is his. What once was estrangement from God has now become a form of absolute love because he journeyed through this estrangement more deeply than a mere man could have managed to do: "Love is stronger than hell."

None of this, however, can be understood unless a third moment is considered: seeing the Incarnation of the Word, all of Jesus' activity on earth, and especially his abandonment by God on the Cross as the participatory achievement of the Holy Spirit of Father and Son. This was set forth in greater detail in volume 3 of the *Theo-Logic* and will only be summarized here. If the Spirit is the relation between Father and Son, then he is most so, indeed with extraordinary overabundance, on the Cross. This is so because the Spirit both reveals as well as effects the most extreme "separation" of Father and Son *as* the epiphany of their highest unity, which happens from that transcendental plane where the "holy exchange" takes place.

This insight then opens out to another: as the Spirit of the Son breathed out onto the world, he comes into contact with individual finite freedom from this position. In other words, he does not do so externally, which would be impossible for someone endowed with freedom: rather, the Spirit breathes from where every created freedom—whether open or closed to God—has its origin and its constitution: in its orientation for the authentically good and, through this, in its drive to realize itself as freedom.

As was already pointed out above, from this point of origin the Spirit confronts the finite and deficient freedom with itself and shows to it that it can truly be a freedom that finds fulfillment. What the Spirit accomplishes from the Cross is to work effects in that region of the finite spirit where the finite form is given first of all to itself (whether in the form of *gratia actualis adjuvans* or a grace already *sanctificans* need not be discussed here, since the difference between actual and sanctifying grace only comes into play in the fourth moment, when a person either accepts or rejects grace). There is no room for extrinsicism here! There only remains the question of whether the finite spirit deigns to recognize that it must receive its own existence in order to be and whether, in those cases where it is a spirit estranged from God, it will convert to this primal fact—both to itself and to God.

There is a great deal we could say in detail about the connection between the second and third moment: Jesus' death in the sinner's estrangement from God means that no sinner can now attain to a perfect "autonomous" loneliness. This is a death of ultimate surrender to the Father and to us, consummated from within the surrender of his (Holy) Spirit exhaled in death and inhaled into the world at Easter. The event depicted as the third moment is indissolubly bound up with the second, both historically and meta-historically. This also shows that the feast of Pentecost is inconceivable without that of Corpus Christi.

But there still remains the fourth moment: the Yes or No of finite freedom to the solicitation of the Spirit at the very roots of that freedom. Here all human forms of knowing cease: "I do not even judge myself. . . . It is the Lord who judges me" (1 Cor 4:3). We do not know whether a human freedom can deny to the very end this offer of the Spirit to give it his own true freedom. If it could do so definitively, then it would be fully conscious in doing so and would be committing the sin against the Holy Spirit, an "eternal sin" that "never has forgiveness" (Mk 3:29).

There is only room for hope at this point, where we simply can know nothing more. For a Christian, this is no arbitrary hope but one that makes, according to Jesus' command of love, no exception of any of our fellow human beings and lets none of them travel but halfway to the goal and then falter. "J'espère en Toi pour nous" (Gabriel Marcel: I hope in Thee for us). We have the *obligation* to hope for the salvation of all.[1] "The funda-

---

[1] Karl Rahner, *Sacramentum Mundi* II, 737.

mental referent to this sense of salvation in dogmatic theology
—that there is a real possibility of eternal catastrophe—must set
the boundary marker and be for us a kind of inner Ariadne's
thread whenever we begin to speculate on this theme."[2] All we
can finally do is simply ask: "Will it really be *everyone* who can
be reconciled? No theology or prophecy can answer this question. But love *hopes for everything* (1 Cor 13:7). I cannot do otherwise than hope for the reconciliation of all men in Christ.
Such unlimited hope is not only permitted to the Christian, it
is *commanded*."[3]

---

[2] Joseph Ratzinger, *Lexikon für Theologie und Kirche*, 448.
[3] Hermann-Joseph Lauter, *Pastoralblatt* (1982), 101.